JOHN LOGAN received ᵤₙ̱   er
Critic Circle and Drama League awaras ᵢₙ̱   ₑd,
directed by Michael Grandage. This play premiered at
the Donmar Warehouse in London and at the Golden
Theatre on Broadway. Since then *Red* has had more than
200 productions across the US and has been presented
in over thirty countries. In 2013, his play *Peter and Alice*
premiered in London and *I'll Eat You Last: A Chat with
Sue Mengers* opened on Broadway. He co-wrote (with
Brian Yorkey) the book for the musical *The Last Ship*,
composed by Sting and directed by Joe Mantello. He is
also the author of more than a dozen other plays including
Never the Sinner and *Hauptmann*. As a screenwriter, Logan
has been three times nominated for the Oscar® and has
received a Golden Globe®, BAFTA and WGA Award.
His film work includes *Skyfall, Spectre, Hugo, The Aviator,
Gladiator, Rango, Coriolanus, Sweeney Todd, The Last Samurai,
Any Given Sunday* and *RKO 281*. He created and executive
produces *Penny Dreadful* for Showtime.

JOHNPLAYS
LOGANONE

RED

PETER AND ALICE

I'LL EAT YOU LAST

OBERON BOOKS
LONDON

WWW.OBERONBOOKS.COM

First published in 2016 by Oberon Books Ltd
521 Caledonian Road, London N7 9RH
Tel: +44 (0) 20 7607 3637 / Fax: +44 (0) 20 7607 3629
e-mail: info@oberonbooks.com
www.oberonbooks.com

A catalogue record for this book is available from the British
Library.

PB ISBN: 9781783198528
E ISBN: 9781783198535

Cover design by James Illman

Converted by CPI Group (UK) Ltd, Croydon, CR0 4YY.

Contents

Foreword

The first time I met John Logan he was ready to pitch. L.A.-based and with Academy Award nominations already under his belt, he wanted to talk about the new play he'd sent me. The play was *Red* and I knew I wanted to direct it the moment I'd read it so, really, it was me who should have been pitching to him.

John Logan is the kind of playwright directors and producers spend a lifetime looking for. He takes his inspiration from real life and introduces a narrative that allows that life to be magnified and touch us all. He delves so deeply into the lives of his characters, he makes us question ourselves. The frail, investigating mind of Peter Llewelyn Davies in *Peter and Alice* is a perfect example of Logan's ability to take the essence of someone and go far deeper than it is possible to imagine. His truth has an honesty that mark him out. There is no compromise in Logan's writing, no censorship. People say what they think and he expects his audience to go there.

Having directed the world premiere of two of the plays in this edition I can confidently state that he writes truly great parts for actors. They love saying his lines. He seems to have a deep understanding of what they need and something happens in performance that doesn't even happen on the page. He also has a deep understanding of what audiences need and enjoys creating emotionally charged theatre that lingers in the mind long after the event.

There is no life long enough for John Logan. If he lives to be a hundred and ten, he won't get everything done. Nowhere near. He has the most febrile imagination of anyone I've ever worked with and he understands the only way to survive is to keep on walking – metaphorically and literally (he relaxes by going on long hikes – no spas for him). He has the energy of the Rothko he created in *Red* and the determination of the Sue Mengers he created in *I'll Eat You Last*. He is *all* of his characters. He is a force of nature. For readers who are coming to his work for the first time, this book is an unexploded bomb. Enjoy.

Michael Grandage
London, 2015

RED

Red was first performed at Donmar Warehouse, London on 3 December 2009, with the following cast and creative team:

ROTHKO	Alfred Molina
KEN	Eddie Redmayne

Creative Team

Director	Michael Grandage
Designer	Christopher Oram
Lighting Designer	Neil Austin
Composer and Sound Designer	Adam Cork

Red was first performed on Broadway at Golden Theatre, New York on 11 March 2010, with the following cast:

ROTHKO	Alfred Molina
KEN	Eddie Redmayne
ROTHKO UNDERSTUDY	Stephen Rowe
KEN UNDERSTUDY	Gabriel Ebert

Creative Team

Director	Michael Grandage
Set and Costume Designer	Christopher Oram
Lighting Designer	Neil Austin
Composer and Sound Designer	Adam Cork

New York Producers
Arielle Tepper Madover
Stephanie P. McClelland
Matthew Byam Shaw
Neal Street
Fox Theatricals
Ruth Hendel/Barbara Whitman
Philip Hagemann/Murray Rosenthal
The Donmar Warehouse

Characters

MARK ROTHKO
American painter, 50s or older

KEN
His new assistant, 20s

Setting

Rothko's studio, 222 Bowery, New York City.
Circa 1958-1959.

Rothko's studio is an old gymnasium. The hardwood floor is splattered and stained with hues of dark red paint. There is a cluttered counter or tables filled with buckets of paint, tins of turpentine, tubes of glue, crates of eggs, bottles of Scotch, packets of pigment, coffee cans filled with brushes, a portable burner or stovetop, and a phone. There is also a phonograph with messy stacks of records.

There is one door leading to an unseen vestibule where the characters change into their work clothes and enter and exit the studio.

Most importantly, representations of some of Rothko's magnificent Seagram Mural paintings are stacked and displayed around the room. Rothko had a pulley system that could raise, lower and display several of the paintings simultaneously. The paintings could be repositioned throughout the play, with a different arrangement for each scene.

There is also an imaginary painting 'hanging' right in front of the audience, which Rothko studies throughout the play.

Alternately, the entire setting could be abstract.

Dedicated to Stephen Sondheim
for reminding me.

SCENE ONE

ROTHKO stands, staring forward.

He is looking directly at the audience. (He is actually studying one of his Seagram Mural paintings, which hangs before him.)

Pause.

ROTHKO lights a cigarette. He wears thick glasses and old, ill-fitting clothes spattered with specks of glue and paint.

Contemplative classical music is playing on a phonograph.

ROTHKO takes a drag on his cigarette.

Pause.

There is the sound of a door opening and closing from the unseen entry vestibule offstage.

KEN, a man in his early 20s, enters nervously. He wears a suit and tie. This is the first time he has been in the studio. He looks around.

He is about to speak.

ROTHKO gestures for him not to speak. Then he beckons for KEN to join him.

KEN goes to ROTHKO, stands next to him.

ROTHKO indicates the central painting; the audience.

ROTHKO: What do you see?

KEN is about to respond –

ROTHKO: Wait. Stand closer. You've got to get close. Let it pulsate. Let it work on you. Closer. Too close. There. Let it spread out. Let it wrap its arms around you; let it *embrace* you, filling even your peripheral vision so nothing else exists or has ever existed or will ever exist. Let the picture do its work – But work with it. Meet it halfway for God's sake! Lean forward, lean into it. Engage with it!… Now, what do you see? – Wait, wait, wait!

7

He hurries and lowers the lighting a bit, then returns to KEN.

ROTHKO: So, now, what do you see? – Be specific. No, be exact. Be exact – but sensitive. You understand? Be kind. Be a human being, that's all I can say. Be a *human being* for once in your life! These pictures deserve compassion and they live or die in the eye of the sensitive viewer, they quicken only if the empathetic viewer will let them. That is what they cry out for. That is why they where created. That is what they deserve… Now… What do you see?

Beat.

KEN: Red.

ROTHKO: But do you *like* it?

KEN: Mm.

ROTHKO: Speak up.

KEN: Yes.

ROTHKO: Of course you *like* it – how can you not *like* it?! Everyone likes everything nowadays. They like the television and the phonograph and the soda pop and the shampoo and the Cracker Jack. Everything becomes everything else and it's all nice and pretty and *likable.* Everything is fun in the sun! Where's the discernment? Where's the arbitration that separates what I *like* from what I *respect,* what I deem *worthy,* what has…listen to me now…*significance.*

ROTHKO moves and turns up the lights again, although he keeps them relatively low, and then switches off the record player, as he continues.

ROTHKO: Maybe this is a dinosaur talking. Maybe I'm a dinosaur sucking up the oxygen from you cunning little mammals hiding in the bushes waiting to take over. Maybe I'm speaking a lost language unknown to your generation. But a generation that does not aspire to seriousness, to meaning, is unworthy to walk in the shadow of those who have gone before, I mean those who have struggled and surmounted, I mean those who have aspired, I mean Rembrandt, I mean Turner, I mean Michelangelo and Matisse… I mean obviously Rothko.

He stares at KEN, challenging.

ROTHKO: Do you aspire?

KEN: Yes.

ROTHKO: To what? To what do you aspire?

KEN: I want to be a painter so I guess I aspire to…painting.

ROTHKO: Then those clothes won't do. We work here. Hang up your jacket outside. I appreciate you put on your Sunday clothes to impress me, it's poignant really, touches me, but it's ridiculous. We work hard here; this isn't a goddamn Old World salon with tea cakes and lemonade. Go hang up your jacket outside.

KEN exits to the entry vestibule off stage. He returns without his jacket. Takes off his tie and rolls up his sleeves.

ROTHKO: Sidney told you what I need here?

KEN: Yes.

ROTHKO busies himself, sorting brushes, arranging canvases, etc., as:

ROTHKO: We start every morning at nine and work until five. Just like bankers. You'll help me stretch the canvases and mix the paints and clean the brushes and build the stretchers and move the paintings and also help apply the ground color – which is *not* painting, so any lunatic assumptions you make in that direction you need to banish immediately. You'll pick up food and cigarettes and anything else I want, any whim, no matter how demanding or demeaning. If you don't like that, leave right now. Answer me. Yes or no.

KEN: Yes.

ROTHKO: Consider: I am not your rabbi, I am not your father, I am not your shrink, I am not your friend, I am not your teacher – I am your employer. You understand?

KEN: Yes.

ROTHKO: As my assistant you will see many things here, many ingenious things. But they're all secret. You cannot talk about any of this. Don't think I don't have enemies because I do and I don't just mean the other painters and gallery owners and museum curators and goddamn-son-of-a-bitch-art-critics, not to mention that vast panoply of disgruntled viewers who loathe me and my work because they do not have the heart, nor the patience, nor the capacity, to think, to *understand*, because they are not *human beings*, like we talked about, you remember?

KEN: Yes.

ROTHKO: I'm painting a series of murals now – *(He gestures all around.)* – I'll probably do thirty or forty and then choose which work best, in concert, like a fugue. You'll help me put on the undercoat and then I'll paint them and then I'll look at them and then paint some more. I do a lot of layers, one after another, like a glaze, slowly building the image, like pentimento, letting the luminescence emerge until it's done.

KEN: How do you know when it's done?

ROTHKO: There's tragedy in every brush stroke.

KEN: Ah.

ROTHKO: Swell. Let's have a drink.

ROTHKO pours two glasses of Scotch. He hands one to KEN.

They drink. KEN is unused to drinking so early in the morning.

Beat.

ROTHKO stares at him, appraising.

ROTHKO: Answer me a question… Don't think about it, just
    say the first thing that comes into your head. No cognition.

KEN: Okay.

ROTHKO: You ready?

KEN: Yeah.

ROTHKO: Who's your favourite painter?

KEN: Jackson Pollock.

ROTHKO: *(Wounded.)* Ah.

KEN: Sorry.

ROTHKO: No, no –

KEN: Let me do it again.

ROTHKO: No –

KEN: Come on –

ROTHKO: No, it's silly –

KEN: Come on, ask me again.

ROTHKO: Who's your favourite painter?

KEN: Picasso.

KEN laughs.

ROTHKO doesn't.

ROTHKO glowers at him.

KEN's laugh dies.

ROTHKO roams.

ROTHKO: Hmm, Pollock… Always Pollock. Don't get me
    wrong, he was a great painter, we came up together, I
    knew him very well.

KEN: What was he like?

ROTHKO: You read Nietzsche?

KEN: What?

ROTHKO: You ever read Nietzsche? *The Birth of Tragedy*?

KEN: No.

ROTHKO: You call yourself an artist? One can't discuss Pollock without it. One can't discuss anything without it. What do they teach you in art school now?

KEN: I –

ROTHKO: You ever read Freud?

KEN: No –

ROTHKO: Jung?

KEN: Well –

ROTHKO: Byron? Wordsworth? Aeschylus? Turgenev? Sophocles? Schopenhauer? Shakespeare? *Hamlet*? At least *Hamlet*, please God! Quote me *Hamlet*. Right now.

KEN: 'To be or not to be, that is the question.'

ROTHKO: Is that the question?

KEN: I don't know.

ROTHKO: You have a lot to learn, young man. Philosophy. Theology. Literature. Poetry. Drama. History. Archeology. Anthropology. Mythology. Music. These are your tools as much as brush and pigment. You cannot be an *artist* until you are civilized. You cannot be *civilized* until you learn. To be civilized is to know where you belong in the continuum of your art and your world. To surmount the past, you must know the past.

KEN: I thought you weren't my teacher.

ROTHKO: You should be so blessed I talk to you about art.

ROTHKO moves away.

12

Beat.

ROTHKO: How do you feel?

KEN: How do I feel?

ROTHKO indicates the huge mural paintings all around them.

ROTHKO: How do *they* make you feel?

KEN: Give me a second.

KEN moves to the middle of the room and takes in all the paintings.

ROTHKO: So?

KEN: Give me a second.

Beat.

KEN: Disquieted.

ROTHKO: And?

KEN: Thoughtful.

ROTHKO: And?

KEN: Um… Sad.

ROTHKO: *Tragic.*

KEN: Yeah.

ROTHKO: They're for a restaurant.

KEN: What?

ROTHKO: They're for a restaurant.

ROTHKO smiles. He enjoys this.

ROTHKO: So I'm minding my own business when Mister Philip Johnson calls me. You know Mister Philip Johnson, the world-renowned architect?

KEN: Not personally.

ROTHKO: Of course you don't know him personally, you
    don't know anyone personally. Don't interrupt. Mister
    Philip Johnson calls me. He's designing the new Seagram
    Building on Park Avenue, he and Mies van der Rohe.
    These are names with which to conjure, are they not?
    Philip Johnson and Mies van der Rohe, titans of their field,
    revolutionists. Together they are making a building unlike
    anything the world has yet seen, reflecting the golden
    ambitions of not only this city and its inhabitants but of all
    mankind. In this building there is to be a restaurant called
    the Four Seasons, like the Vivaldi, and on the walls of this
    restaurant…

He gestures expansively to his paintings.

Beat.

ROTHKO: *(Proud.)* Thirty-five thousand dollars they are paying
    me. No other painter comes close.

*KEN is impressed. Thirty-five thousand dollars is a fortune. Call it two
million dollars in today's money.*

ROTHKO walks to the center of the room, filling himself with the work.

ROTHKO: My first murals… Imagine a frieze all around the
    room, a continuous narrative filling the walls, one to
    another, each a new chapter, the story unfolding, look and
    they are there, inescapable and inexorable, like doom.

KEN: Are these ones done?

ROTHKO: They're in process. I have to study them now.

KEN: Study them?

ROTHKO: Most of painting is thinking. Didn't they teach you
    that? Ten percent is putting paint onto the canvas. The rest
    is waiting.

ROTHKO takes in his paintings.

ROTHKO: All my life I wanted just this, my friend: to
    create a *place*… A place where the viewer could live in

contemplation with the work and give it some of the same attention and care I gave it. Like a chapel... A place of communion.

KEN: But...it's a restaurant.

ROTHKO: No... I will make it a temple.

Beat.

ROTHKO is lost in his paintings.

KEN watches him for a moment.

Then he moves to the phonograph. He turns it on, lowers the needle. The classical music plays.

He studies ROTHKO.

SCENE TWO

ROTHKO stands starting at the central painting; the audience.

Classical music plays from the phonograph. (ROTHKO favoured Mozart and Schubert.)

KEN enters. He carries bags of Chinese takeout food. He now wears work clothes splattered with paint and glue. Months have passed and he is more comfortable here.

KEN puts a handful of change into an empty coffee can and then unloads the cartons of food.

ROTHKO muses.

ROTHKO: Rembrandt and Rothko... Rembrandt and Rothko... Rothko and Rembrandt... Rothko and Rembrandt... And Turner. Rothko and Rembrandt and Turner... Rothko and Rembrandt and Turner –

KEN: – Oh my.

Beat.

ROTHKO lights a cigarette.

KEN: The Chinese place is closing.

ROTHKO: Everything worthwhile ends. We are in the perpetual process now: creation, maturation, cessation.

KEN: There's another Chinese round the corner.

ROTHKO: The eternal cycles grind on, generations pass away, hope turns arid, but there's another Chinese round the corner.

KEN: Not much for small talk.

ROTHKO: It's small.

He joins KEN. He stands and eats Chinese food messily with a fork through the following.

KEN: I went to the Modern last night, saw the Picasso show.

ROTHKO: And?

KEN: I don't think he's so much concerned with generations passing away.

ROTHKO: Don't kid yourself, kid. That man – though now a charlatan of course signing menus for money like Dali, when he's not making ugly little pots, also for money – that man at his best understood the workings of time… Where's the receipt?

KEN gives him the receipt for the Chinese food.

ROTHKO puts it into a shoebox filled with other receipts as he continues without stopping.

ROTHKO: Tragic, really, to grow superfluous in your own lifetime. We destroyed Cubism, de Kooning and me and Pollock and Barnett Newman and all the others. We stomped it to death. Nobody can paint a Cubist picture today.

KEN: You take pride in that. 'Stomping' Cubism to death.

ROTHKO: The child must banish the father. Respect him, but kill him.

KEN: And enjoy it?

ROTHKO: Doesn't matter. Just be audacious and do it...
Courage in painting isn't facing the blank canvas, it's facing Manet, it's facing Velasquez. All we can do is move beyond what was there, to what is here, and hope to get some intimation of what will be here. 'What is past and passing and to come.' That's Yeats, whom you haven't read.

KEN: Come on, but Picasso –

ROTHKO tries another carton of food, keeps eating.

ROTHKO: Picasso I thank for teaching me that movement is everything! Movement is life. The second we're born we squall, we writhe, we squirm; to live is to move. Without movement paintings are what?

KEN: Dead?

ROTHKO: Precisely... *(He gestures to his paintings.)* Look at the *tension* between the blocks of color: the dark and the light, the red and the black and the brown. They exist in a state of flux – of movement. They abut each other on the actual canvas, so too do they abut each other in your eye. They ebb and flow and shift, gently pulsating. The more you look at them the more they move... They float in space, they breathe... Movement, communication, gesture, flux, interaction; letting them work... They're not dead because they're not static. They move through space if you let them, this movement takes time, so they're temporal. They require *time.*

KEN: They demand it. They don't work without it.

ROTHKO: This is why it's so important to me to create a *place.* A place the viewer can contemplate the paintings over time and let them move.

KEN: *(Excited.)* They *need* the viewer. They're not like representational pictures, like traditional landscapes or portraits.

ROTHKO: Tell me why.

KEN: Because they *change*, they move, they pulse. Representational pictures are unchanging; they don't require the active participation of the viewer. Go to the Louvre in the middle of the night and the 'Mona Lisa' will still be smiling. But do these paintings still pulse when they're alone?

KEN is lost in thought.

ROTHKO watches him, pleased.

KEN: That's why you keep the lights so low.

ROTHKO: Is it?

KEN: To help the illusion. Like a magician. Like a play. To keep it mysterious, to let the pictures pulsate. Turn on bright lights and the stage effect is ruined – suddenly it's nothing but a bare stage with a bunch of fake walls.

KEN goes to the light switches. He snaps on all the lights. Ugly fluorescent lights sizzle on. The room immediately loses its magic.

ROTHKO: What do you see?

KEN: My eyes are adjusting… Just… White.

ROTHKO: What does white make you think of?

KEN: Bones, skeletons… Charnel house… Anemia… Cruelty.

ROTHKO is surprised by this response.

ROTHKO: Really?

KEN: It's like an operating theatre now.

ROTHKO: How does white make you *feel*?

KEN: Frightened?

ROTHKO: Why?

KEN: Doesn't matter.

ROTHKO: Why?

KEN: It's like the snow…outside the room where my parents died. It was winter. I remember the snow outside the window: white… *(Turns his attention to the paintings.)* And the pictures in this light… They're flat. Vulgar… This light hurts them.

ROTHKO turns off the fluorescent lights.

The normal light returns.

ROTHKO: You see how it is with them? How vulnerable they are?… People think I'm controlling: controlling the light; controlling the height of the pictures; controlling the shape of the gallery… It's not controlling, it's *protecting*. A picture lives by companionship. It dies by the same token. It's a risky act to send it out into the world.

KEN tosses away the cartons of food and straightens up.

ROTHKO puts on a new classical record. Moves back to studying his central painting.

A beat as the mood settles.

KEN: You ever paint outdoors?

ROTHKO: You mean out in nature?

KEN: Yeah.

ROTHKO: Nature doesn't work for me. The light's no good.

KEN is amused.

ROTHKO: All those bugs – ach! I know, those *plein air* painters, they sing to you endless paeans about the majesty of natural sunlight. Get out there and muck around in the grass, they tell you, like a cow. When I was young I didn't know any better so I would haul my supplies out there and the wind would blow the paper and the easel would fall over and the ants would get in the paint. Oy… But then I go to Rome for the first time. I go to the Santa Maria del Popolo to see Caravaggio's 'Conversion of Saul,' which turns out is tucked away in a dark corner of this dark church with no natural light. It's like a cave. But the painting *glowed*! With a sort of *rapture* it glowed. Consider: Caravaggio was commissioned to paint the picture for this specific place, he had no choice. He stands there and he looks around. It's like under the ocean it's so goddamn dark. How's he going to paint here? He turns to his creator: 'God, help me, unworthy sinner that I am. Tell me, O Lord on High, what the fuck do I do now?!'

KEN laughs.

ROTHKO: Then it comes to him: the divine spark. He illuminates the picture from *within*! He gives it *inner* luminosity. It *lives*… Like one of those bioluminescent fish from the bottom of the ocean, radiating its own effulgence. You understand? Caravaggio was –

He abruptly stops.

KEN looks at him.

Beat.

ROTHKO stares at his painting.

He tilts his head.

Like he's listening.

Like he's seeing something new in the painting.

ROTHKO: Bring me the second bucket.

KEN, excited, brings him a brush and a bucket of dark, maroon paint.

KEN: Are you really going to paint?

ROTHKO: What the hell do you think I *have* been doing?!

KEN retreats.

He watches ROTHKO closely.

ROTHKO dips the five-inch housepainter's brush into the paint.

He's ready.

Then he stands there, frozen.

Just his eyes move craftily over the canvas.

Paint drips.

KEN is breathless.

ROTHKO is coiled.

He tilts his head, studying, adjudicating.

He considers the color of the paint in the bucket. Needs something.

ROTHKO: Gimme black number four and the first maroon.

KEN brings some powdered pigments in old jars.

ROTHKO instructs, still barely moving. His eyes dart from the bucket of paint to the canvas.

ROTHKO: A pinch of black.

KEN adds a bit of black pigment, stirs it carefully.

ROTHKO: Just that amount again.

KEN adds a bit more, keeps stirring.

ROTHKO: Twice as much maroon.

KEN adds some maroon pigment, keeps stirring.

ROTHKO is unsure.

He looks at the painting.

The moment is passing.

He is getting desperate.

ROTHKO: *(To himself, frustrated.)* Come on…come on…come on… What does it need?

KEN: Red.

ROTHKO: I wasn't talking to you!

Beat.

Tragically, the moment has passed for ROTHKO.

He FLINGS the paintbrush away. It splatters.

He spins on KEN.

ROTHKO: DON'T YOU EVER DO THAT AGAIN!

He rages, stomping restlessly around the room.

ROTHKO: By what right do you speak?! By what right do you express an opinion on my work? Who the fuck are you? What have you done? What have you seen? Where have you earned the right to exist here with me and these things you don't understand?! 'RED?!' You want to paint the thing?! Go ahead – here's red–!

He clumsily slings packets of various red paints at KEN.

ROTHKO: And red! And red! And red! – I don't even know what that means! What does 'red' mean to me? You mean scarlet? You mean crimson? You mean plum-mulberry-magenta-burgundy-salmon-carmine-carnelian-coral? Anything but 'red!' What is 'RED?!'

ROTHKO stands, getting his breath, collecting himself.

Beat.

KEN picks up the packets of paint from the floor.

ROTHKO prowls, discontent.

Pause.

KEN: I meant sunrise.

ROTHKO: Sunrise?

KEN: I meant the red at sunrise… The feeling of it.

ROTHKO: *(Derisive.)* Oh, the 'feeling of it.'

Beat.

KEN continues to clean up, clearing away the bucket of paint and brush.

Beat.

ROTHKO: What do you mean the feeling of it?

KEN: I didn't mean red paint only. I meant the *emotion* of red at sunrise.

ROTHKO: Sunrise isn't red.

KEN: Yes it is.

ROTHKO: I'm telling you it's not.

KEN: Sunrise is red and red is sunrise.

KEN keeps cleaning up.

KEN: Red is heart beat. Red is passion. Red wine. Red roses. Red lipstick. Beets. Tulips. Peppers.

ROTHKO: Arterial blood.

KEN: That too.

ROTHKO thinks about it.

ROTHKO: Rust on the bike on the lawn.

KEN: And apples… And tomatoes.

ROTHKO: Dresden firestorm at night. The sun in Rousseau, the flag in Delacroix, the robe in El Greco.

KEN: A rabbit's nose. An albino's eyes. A parakeet.

ROTHKO: Florentine marble. Atomic flash. Nick yourself shaving, blood in the Barbasol.

KEN: The Ruby Slippers. Technicolor. That phone to the Kremlin on the President's desk.

ROTHKO: Russian flag, Nazi flag, Chinese flag.

KEN: Persimmons. Pomegranates. Red Light District. Red tape. Rouge.

ROTHKO: Lava. Lobsters. Scorpions.

KEN: Stop sign. Sports car. A blush.

ROTHKO: Viscera. Flame. Dead Fauvists.

KEN: Traffic lights. Titian hair.

ROTHKO: Slash your wrists. Blood in the sink.

KEN: Santa Claus.

ROTHKO: Satan.

Beat.

ROTHKO: So…red.

KEN: Exactly.

ROTHKO gazes thoughtfully at his painting.

ROTHKO: We got more cigarettes?

KEN gets a pack of cigarettes from a drawer and tosses them to ROTHKO.

ROTHKO opens them and lights one as:

ROTHKO: More than anything, you know what?

KEN: What?

ROTHKO: Matisse's painting 'The Red Studio.' It's a picture of his own studio; the walls are a brilliant red, the floor and furniture, all red, like the color had radiated out of him and swallowed everything up. When the Modern first put that picture up I would spend hours looking at it. Day after day I would go… You could argue that everything I do today, you can trace the bloodlines back to that painting

24

and those hours standing there, letting the painting work, allowing it to *move*... The more I looked at it the more it pulsated around me, I was totally saturated, it swallowed me... Such *plains* of red he made, such energetic blocks of color, such emotion!

Beat.

ROTHKO sits in an old arm chair, staring at the central painting. Exhausted and depressed.

KEN senses the change in ROTHKO's mood.

ROTHKO takes off his thick glasses, cleans them on his shirt as:

ROTHKO: That was a long time ago.

KEN: It's still there.

ROTHKO: I can't look at it now.

KEN: Why?

ROTHKO: It's too depressing.

KEN: How can all that red be depressing?

ROTHKO: I don't see the red any more... Even in that painting, that total and profound immersion in red...it's there. The mantel above a dresser, just over the centerline, set off by yellow of all goddamn things. He wanted it inescapable.

KEN: What?

ROTHKO: Black.

KEN: The color black?

ROTHKO: The thing black.

Beat.

ROTHKO: There is only one thing I fear in life, my friend... One day the black will swallow the red.

He puts on his glasses again and stares at his painting.

25

SCENE THREE

KEN is alone. He is at a stove or burner, gently heating and stirring liquid in a large pot. This mixture will be the base layer for a new blank canvas.

A small painting, wrapped in brown paper, is tucked unobtrusively in a corner.

He talks on the phone as he stirs.

KEN: *(On phone.)* …that's easy for you to say, you don't know him… *(He glances to the wrapped painting.)* … I'll show it to him if I think the moment's right. He knows I'm a painter, he's got to be expecting it… No, no it depends on his mood … don't tell me what to do! You're just like him…

He hears the sounds of ROTHKO entering outside.

KEN: He's here. I'll tell you how it goes. Pray for me.

He hangs up.

> *ROTHKO enters with some supplies for the base layer. He does not notice the wrapped painting.*

KEN: Good morning.

ROTHKO: Morning. I got the other maroon… I'll take over, you finish the canvas.

ROTHKO goes to the pot and takes over stirring. He adds some new maroon pigment to the mixture. Like concocting a witch's brew, he also stirs in glue, chemicals, chalk, raw eggs and other powdered pigments.

KEN works on tightening and stapling a blank canvas. It is square, about six feet by six feet or larger.

ROTHKO: I went by the Seagram building last night, it's coming along.

KEN: How's the restaurant?

ROTHKO: Still under construction, but they took me around, got a sense of it.

KEN: And?

ROTHKO: Too much natural light, as always, but it'll work. You'll be able to see the murals from the main dining room… I made some sketches; I'll find them for you.

KEN: You ever worry it's not the right place for them?

ROTHKO: How can it not be the right place for them when they are being created specifically for that place? Sometimes your logic baffles me.

ROTHKO goes to the phonograph and flips through the records.

KEN glances again to his wrapped painting. Is this the time to bring it up? No. He doesn't have the nerve quite yet.

ROTHKO picks a classical record and puts it on.

Then he returns to stirring the mixture.

Beat.

KEN: So I read Nietzsche. *Birth of Tragedy* like you said.

ROTHKO: Like I said?

KEN: You said if I wanted to know about Jackson Pollock I had to read *The Birth of Tragedy.*

ROTHKO: I said that?

KEN: Yeah.

ROTHKO: I don't remember. It's very like something I would say.

KEN: So what about Pollock?

ROTHKO: First tell me what you make of the book.

KEN: Interesting.

ROTHKO: That's like saying 'red.' Don't be enigmatic; you're too young to be enigmatic.

KEN: I think I know why you wanted me to read it.

ROTHKO: Why?

KEN: Because you see yourself as Apollo and you see him as Dionysus.

ROTHKO: Don't be so pedestrian. Think more.

ROTHKO adds turpentine to the mixture, checks the consistency by letting it run off his paint stirrer. He wants it thin, like a glaze.

KEN stops working.

KEN: Dionysus is the God of wine and excess; of movement and transformation. This is Pollock: wild; rebellious; drunken and unrestrained. The raw experience itself… Apollo is the God of order, method and boundaries. This is Rothko: intellectual; rabbinical; sober and restrained. The raw experience leavened by contemplation… He splatters paint. You study it… He's Dionysus and you're Apollo.

ROTHKO: Exactly right but for entirely missing the point.

KEN: How so?

ROTHKO: You miss the tragedy. The point is always the tragedy.

KEN: For you.

ROTHKO: You think human beings can be divided up so neatly into character types? You think the multifarious complexities and nuances of the psyche – evolving through countless generations, perverted and demented through social neurosis and personal anguish, moulded by faith and lack of faith – can really be so goddamn simple? Pollock is Emotion and Rothko is Intellect? You embarrass yourself… Think more.

KEN thinks as he continues to work on the canvas.

ROTHKO continues to stir the paint, occasionally glancing at KEN.

KEN stops.

KEN: Maybe it's like one of your paintings.

ROTHKO: Most things are. How?

KEN: Dark and light, order and chaos, existing at the same time in the same plain, pulsing back and forth… We pulse too; we're subjects of both Apollo *and* Dionysus, not one or the other. We ebb and flow, like the colors in your pictures, the ecstasy of the Dionysian at war with the restraint of the Apollonian.

ROTHKO: Not at war.

KEN: Not at war?

ROTHKO: It's not really conflict. More like symbiosis.

KEN: They need each other. Dionysus' passion is focused – is made bearable – by Apollo's will to form. In fact the only way we can *endure* the sheer ferocity of Dionysus' emotion is because we have the control and intelligence of Apollo, otherwise the emotion would overwhelm us… So back and forth we go, myth to myth, pulsating.

ROTHKO: And the perfect life would be perfectly balanced between the two, everlastingly on the fulcrum. But our *tragedy* is that we can never achieve that balance. We exist – all of us, for all time – in a state of perpetual dissonance… We long for the raw truth of emotion, but can only endure it with the cool lie of reason… We seek to capture the ephemeral, the miraculous, and put it onto canvas, stopping time but, like an entomologist pinning a butterfly, it dies when we try…. We're foolish that way, we human beings… We try to make the red black.

KEN: But the black is always there, like the mantle in Matisse.

ROTHKO: Like the snow outside the window. It never goes away. Once glimpsed, we can't help being preoccupied with it for the intimations of our mortality are… *(He gestures: everywhere.)* … But still we go on, clinging to that tiny bit of hope – that red – that makes the rest endurable.

KEN: Or just less unendurable.

ROTHKO: That's my friend Jackson Pollock. Finally it was just unendurable.

KEN: What do you mean?

ROTHKO: His suicide.

KEN: He didn't commit suicide.

ROTHKO: Didn't he?

KEN thinks about this as he continues to tighten the canvas.

ROTHKO isn't satisfied with the music. He puts on a different classical record. He listens for a moment and then returns to stirring the mixture.

KEN: Jackson Pollock died in a car accident.

ROTHKO: A man spends years getting drunk, day after day, hammered. Then he gets into an Oldsmobile convertible and races around these little country roads like a lunatic. You tell me what that is if not a lazy suicide... Believe me, when I commit suicide there won't be any doubt about it. No mysterious crumpled car in a ditch, did he or didn't he, it gives me a headache it's so boring.

KEN: 'When' you commit suicide?

ROTHKO: What?

KEN: You said 'When I commit suicide.'

ROTHKO: No I didn't.

KEN: You did.

ROTHKO: You misheard... Let me tell you one thing about your hero, that man really confronted his tragedy. He was valiant in the face of it, he endured as long as he could, then he tried to recede from life, but how could he? He was Jackson Pollock.

KEN: What was his tragedy?

ROTHKO: He became famous.

KEN: Don't be glib.

ROTHKO: His muse evacuated. He grew tired of his form. He grew tired of himself. He lost faith in his viewers... Take your pick... He no longer believed there were any real human beings out there to look at pictures.

KEN: How does that happen to a man?

ROTHKO: Better you should ask how occasionally it doesn't happen.

KEN: I mean he's an artist, he's in *Life* magazine, he's young, he's famous, he has money –

ROTHKO: That's exactly it. Here's a schmuck from Wyoming who can paint. Suddenly he's a *commodity*. He's 'Jackson Pollock.' Lemme tell you, kid, that Oldsmobile convertible really did kill him. Not because it crashed, because it *existed*. Why the fuck did Jackson Pollock have an Oldsmobile convertible?

KEN: So artists should starve?

ROTHKO: Yes, artists should starve. Except me.

KEN smiles.

He has completed working on the canvas.

KEN: Take a look.

ROTHKO moves to the canvas, stands over it, carefully studying it, walking around it. He is looking for flaws in the canvas, as:

ROTHKO: You would have loved Jackson. He was a downtown guy, a real Bohemian. No banker's hours for him, believe you me. Every night the drinking and the talking and the fighting and the dancing and the staying up late; like everyone's romantic idea of what an artist ought to be: the anti-Rothko... At his worst you still loved him though; you loved him because he loved art so much... He thought it *mattered*. He thought painting mattered... Does not the

poignancy stop your heart?… How could this story not end
in tragedy?

Beat.

ROTHKO: Goya said, 'We have Art that we may not perish
from Truth.'… Pollock saw some truth. Then he didn't
have art to protect him any more… Who could survive
that?

Beat.

ROTHKO emerges from his thoughts.

He nods to KEN.

*They lift the canvas from the floor, lean it up against a sawhorse, easel
or wall.*

ROTHKO studies it minutely.

*He delicately picks lint from the canvas. He gently blows remnants of
dust away.*

He continues to study the canvas as:

ROTHKO: I was walking up to my house last week and this
couple was passing. Lady looks in the window, says: 'I
wonder who owns all the Rothkos.'… Just like that I'm a
noun. A Rothko.

KEN: A commodity.

ROTHKO: An overmantle.

KEN: A what?

*ROTHKO continues to study the blank canvas for flaws, for discoloration,
for imperfection. He moves closer, he backs all the way up, he moves closer
again, tilting his head back and forth, adjudicating, as:*

ROTHKO: The overmantles. Those paintings doomed to
become *decoration.* You know, over the fireplace in the
penthouse. They say to you, 'I need something to work
with the sofa, you understand. Or something bright and

cheery for the breakfast nook, which is orange, do you have anything in orange? Or burnt-umber? Or sea-foam green? Here's a paint chip from the Sherwin-Williams. And could you cut it down to fit the sideboard?'… Or even worse, 'Darling, I simply *must* have one because my neighbour has one, that social-climbing bitch, in fact if she has one, I need *three*!'… Or even worse, 'I must have one because the New York Times tells me I should have one – or someone told me the New York Times tells me I should have one because who has time to read any more.'… 'Oh, don't make me look at it! I never look at it! It's so depressing!'… 'All those fuzzy rectangles, my kid could do that in kindergarten, it's nothing but a scam, this guy's a fraud.'… Still, they buy it… It's an investment… It's screwing the neighbours… It's buying class… It's buying taste… It goes with the lamp… It's cheaper than a Pollock… It's interior decoration… It's anything but what it is.

Beat.

ROTHKO seems to have accepted the canvas.

ROTHKO: Okey-dokey. Let's prime the canvas.

They work together now.

They have done this many times, it is a well-practised ritual.

They pour the paint/glue mixture from the stove – the base layer for the canvas – into two large buckets. The mixture is a thin liquid, almost a glaze, of dark plum.

They bring the buckets to either side of the six-foot square canvas. They make sure the canvas is secure.

They prepare house painting brushes. ROTHKO rubs his rhythmically across his hand, warming and limbering the bristles.

KEN waits. Ready.

ROTHKO stares intently at the blank canvas.

A long beat as he rubs his brush back and forth across his hand, thinking.

KEN watches him, poised.

Then ROTHKO goes to the phonograph, flips through the stack of records, finds the one he wants, and puts it onto the phonograph.

He lowers the needle. He listens. He lifts the needle again. Finally finds the exact place in the record he is looking for. He lowers the needle.

Spirited classical music plays.

He returns to the canvas.

He nods to KEN.

Ready? Ready.

They dip their brushes.

They are on opposite sides of the canvas.

KEN crouches; he will do the lower half of the canvas.

ROTHKO stands tall; he will do the upper half of the canvas.

KEN waits for ROTHKO to begin.

ROTHKO waits for the music.

With theatrical panache, ROTHKO waits for the exact moment the music thunders most dramatically and then –

He begins to paint –

He moves very quickly –

Using strong, broad strokes he sweeps across the top of the canvas as quickly as possible – big, horizontal gestures – moving fast to make sure the base layer is even and smooth –

KEN does the same for the bottom half of the painting –

Some of ROTHKO's paint drips and splashes down on KEN –

It is like choreography, they move in sync, they move toward each other and then cross, ROTHKO lurching back awkwardly as he continues to paint so KEN can dive in under him gracefully as he continues to paint –

The thin, watery paint splatters and splashes as they dip their brushes and assault the canvas –

It is hard, fast, thrilling work –

The music swells –

And then they are done.

The white canvas is now an even, flat plain of dark plum.

ROTHKO steps back, exhausted, panting for air.

KEN sits heavily on the floor, also exhausted.

Beat.

ROTHKO lights a cigarette.

Then he turns off the phonograph.

KEN rises and cleans himself with a towel. Then he changes his paint-stained shirt.

He begins to straighten up: hauling the buckets away; wiping up the floor; cleaning the brushes.

ROTHKO minutely studies the now-primed canvas.

Then he steps back and back, studies the canvas from across the studio.

ROTHKO: *(Musing.)* So…so…so…it'll do… Maybe it'll do… Possibly adequate… What do you think?

KEN: You mean me? You want me to answer?

ROTHKO: Who else?

KEN: It's a…a good ground, a good base layer. Nice and even.

ROTHKO: We'll see when it dries. Then I can start to paint.

KEN: You really care what I think?

ROTHKO: Not at all.

KEN smiles, continues to clean up.

Then he stops abruptly.

Something about the freshly-primed canvas strikes him.

He stares at it.

Surprisingly, tears come to his eyes. The emotion is unexpected.

ROTHKO: What?

KEN: Nothing…

ROTHKO: What is it?

KEN: It's strange… I'm remembering something… The, um, color…is…

ROTHKO: What?

KEN: Doesn't matter.

ROTHKO: What?

KEN: Dried blood… When the blood dried it got *darker*. On the carpet.

ROTHKO: Which carpet?

KEN: Where my parents died.

KEN tries to shake off the thought. He moves away.

But then he stops again. He can't shake the emotion.

The canvas draws him back.

KEN: It's exactly the color. When the blood dried it got *darker*, that surprised me. I remember being surprised by that…

ROTHKO is intrigued.

ROTHKO: What happened to your parents?

KEN: I don't want to talk about it.

ROTHKO: Yes you do.

KEN: They were murdered.

ROTHKO: Did you say murdered?

KEN: Mm.

ROTHKO: How old were you?

KEN: Seven. This was back in Iowa.

ROTHKO: What happened?

KEN: I honestly don't remember it too well.

ROTHKO: Sure you do.

KEN stares forward, lost in thought.

Beat.

ROTHKO: What do you see?

KEN shakes his head.

ROTHKO: What do you see?

Beat.

KEN: *(Reliving it.)* I woke up…and the first thing I saw was the snow outside my window. I was glad it snowed because it was Saturday and I could go sledding. My Dad would take me sledding, me and my sister. But…but…I didn't smell anything. That was weird. Normally my Mom would be up making breakfast. It was really quiet. I put on my slippers – they were those Neolite ones that look like moccasins. Go into the hall… Now it's really quiet… And it's *cold.* There's a window open somewhere… Then I see my sister, she's just standing in the hallway, staring into my parent's room. The door's open. My sister…she's standing in a puddle of pee. Just staring. Her eyes… I go to the door and look in and see the snow first. Outside the window, so much snow, maybe I'll still go sledding. And then the blood. The bed's stained with it. And the wall. They're on the bed… It was a knife… Apparently it was a knife, I found out later.

Beat.

KEN: Burglars, I found out. At least two of them… But right now I don't know what to do. I just *see*… I… Don't want my sister to see any more. My little sister… I turn around and push her out and shut the door. The door handle… With blood… Is red.

Beat.

KEN: That's all.

ROTHKO: What happened then?

KEN: You mean after that? Um… Nothing really. We went to the neighbours. They called the police.

ROTHKO: What happened to you two?

KEN: State took us. Foster homes. People were nice, actually. They kept us together. But they shuffled us around a lot. We were *rootless*… She's married to a CPA now.

ROTHKO: Rootless?

KEN: Never belonged… Never had a *place*.

ROTHKO: Did they find the guys who did it?

KEN: No. I paint pictures of them sometimes.

Beat.

ROTHKO: You paint pictures of the men who killed your parents?

KEN: Mm. What I imagine them to look like.

ROTHKO: Which is what?

Beat.

KEN: Normal.

Beat.

ROTHKO considers comforting KEN in some way, but doesn't.

He moves away, lights a cigarette.

ROTHKO: When I was a kid in Russia, I saw the Cossacks cutting people up and tossing them into pits… At least I think I remember that, maybe someone told me about it, or I'm just being dramatic, hard to say sometimes.

KEN is relieved that ROTHKO has changed the subject. He continues cleaning up.

KEN: How old were you when you came here?

ROTHKO: Ten. We went to Portland, lived in the ghetto alongside all the other thinky, talky Jews. I was Marcus Rothkowitz then.

KEN: *(Surprised.)* You changed your name?

ROTHKO: My first dealer said he had too many Jewish painters on the books. So Marcus Rothkowitz becomes Mark Rothko. Now nobody knows I'm a Jew!

KEN smiles.

He continues to clean up.

Pause.

KEN: Can I ask you something?

ROTHKO: Can I stop you?

KEN: Are you really scared of black?

ROTHKO: No, I'm really scared of the absence of light.

KEN: Like going blind?

ROTHKO: Like going dead.

KEN: And you equate the color black with death?

ROTHKO: Doesn't everyone?

KEN: I'm asking you.

ROTHKO likes that KEN is pushing back.

ROTHKO: Yes, I equate the color black with the diminution of the life force.

KEN: Black means decay and darkness?

ROTHKO: Doesn't it?

KEN: Because black is the lack of red, if you will.

ROTHKO: Because black is the opposite of red. Not on the spectrum, but in reality.

KEN: I'm talking about in painting.

ROTHKO: Then talk about painting.

KEN: In your pictures the bold colors are the Dionysian element, kept in check by the strict geometric shapes, the Apollonian element. The bright colors are your passion, your will to survive – your 'life force.' But if *black* swallows those bright colors then you lose that excess and extravagance, and what do you have left?

ROTHKO: Go on. I'm fascinated by me.

KEN: *(Undeterred.)* Lose those colors and you have order with no content. You have mathematics with no numbers… Nothing but empty, arid boxes.

ROTHKO: And trust me, as you get older those colors are harder to sustain. The palate fades and we race to catch it before it's gone.

KEN: But…

He stops.

ROTHKO: What?

KEN: Never mind.

ROTHKO: What?

KEN: You'll get mad.

ROTHKO: Me?

KEN: You will.

ROTHKO: And?

KEN: I just think… It's kind of sentimental to equate black with death. That seems an antiquated notion. Sort of *romantic.*

ROTHKO: Romantic?

KEN: I mean…not *honest.*

ROTHKO: Really?

KEN: In reality we both know black's a tool, just like ochre or magenta. It has no affect. Seeing it as malevolent is a weird sort of chromatic anthropomorphising.

ROTHKO: You think so? What about equating white with death; like snow?

KEN: That's different. That's just a personal reaction. I'm not building a whole artistic sensibility around it.

ROTHKO: Maybe you should.

They are growing heated.

KEN: I don't think –

ROTHKO: Use your own life, why not?

KEN: It's not that I –

ROTHKO: Unless you're scared of it.

KEN: I'm not scared.

ROTHKO: Go into all that white.

KEN: I'm not scared, it's just self-indulgent.

ROTHKO: If you say so.

KEN: Not all art has to be psychodrama.

ROTHKO: Doesn't it?

KEN: No.

ROTHKO: You paint pictures of the men who killed your parents.

KEN: That's not *all* I paint.

ROTHKO: Maybe it should be. Then maybe you'd understand what black is.

KEN: Back to that.

ROTHKO: Always.

KEN: At least equating white with death isn't so predictable.

ROTHKO: I'm predictable now?

KEN: Kind of.

ROTHKO: Dishonest and predictable.

KEN: Come on, a painter gets older and the color black starts to infuse his work therefore, the cliché declension goes, he's depressed, he's fearing death, he's losing touch, he's losing relevance, he's saying goodbye.

ROTHKO: That's a cliché except for when it's not.

KEN: But it's not *true.*

ROTHKO: So now you know truth?

KEN: Look at Van Gogh; his last pictures are all color. He goes out and paints the most ecstatic yellows and blues known to man – then shoots himself… Or Matisse, his last works were nothing but great shocks of primary colors.

ROTHKO: You admire those colors.

KEN: Absolutely.

ROTHKO: Why?

KEN: Well, Matisse…he was dying, he knew he was dying, but still he was Matisse. When he got too ill to hold a paint brush he used scissors, cutting up paper and making collages. He never gave up. On his deathbed he was still organizing the color patterns on the ceiling. He had to be who he was.

ROTHKO: And you think *I'm* the romantic! Can't you do any better than that?

He continues, angry and derisive:

ROTHKO: Matisse the Dying Hero, struggling with his last puny gasp to create that final masterpiece… And Jackson Pollock the Beautiful Doomed Youth, dying like Chatterton in his classic Pieta-pose… And Van Gogh, of course Van Gogh, trotted out on all occasions, the ubiquitous symbol for everything, Van Gogh the Misunderstood Martyr – You *insult* these men by reducing them to your own adolescent stereotypes. Grapple with them, yes. Argue with them, always. But don't think you *understand* them. Don't think you have *captured* them. *They are beyond you.*

He moves away, then stops.

ROTHKO: Spend a *lifetime* with them and you might get a moment of insight into their pain… Until then, allow them their grandeur in silence.

ROTHKO returns to studying his central painting.

ROTHKO: Silence is so accurate.

Pause.

ROTHKO seems oblivious to KEN.

KEN continues to clean up for a moment.

Then he stops, looks at his own painting, wrapped in brown paper.

Then he looks at ROTHKO.

KEN unobtrusively picks up his painting and exits briefly. He returns without the painting.

KEN: We need some coffee. Mind if I go out?

ROTHKO: Go on.

KEN gets some money from the coffee can in which they keep petty cash.

He starts to go.

ROTHKO stops him:

ROTHKO: Wait.

ROTHKO looks at him.

ROTHKO: In the National Gallery in London there's a picture by Rembrandt called 'Belshazzar's Feast'… It's an Old Testament story from Daniel: Belshazzar, King of Babylon, is giving a feast and he blasphemes, so a divine hand appears and writes some Hebrew words on the wall as a warning… In the painting these words pulsate from the dark canvas like something miraculous. Rembrandt's Hebrew was atrocious, as you can imagine, but he wrote 'Mene, Mene, Tekel, Upharsin.'… 'You have been weighed in the balance and have been found wanting.'

Beat.

ROTHKO: That's what black is to me… What is it to you?

Beat.

SCENE FOUR

KEN is alone, building a wooden canvas stretcher/frame. He is a good carpenter.

A Chet Baker jazz record plays on the phonograph.

He works quietly.

Beat.

Then the sound of a slamming door from outside surprises him.

ROTHKO rages in, flinging off his overcoat and hat.

ROTHKO: THEY'RE TRYING TO KILL ME! I swear to
God they're trying to kill me! Those prosaic insects!
Those presumptuous, counter-jumping, arriviste SONS-
OF-BITCHES! – These are same goddamn walls where
I hang! You appreciate that?! *My* gallery! *My* walls!
Polluted now beyond sanitation, beyond hygiene, like
the East River, choked with garbage, all that superficial,
meaningless sewage right up there on the wall! The same
sacred space of de Kooning and Motherwell and Smith and
Newman and Pollock and…

He stops.

ROTHKO: What is this music?

KEN: Chet Baker.

ROTHKO: Just when I thought this day couldn't get worse…

KEN: It's jazz.

ROTHKO: Like I care. When you pay the rent, you can pick
the records.

KEN takes the record off.

ROTHKO fumes.

Beat.

KEN: So…how did you like the exhibit?

ROTHKO is not amused.

He lights a cigarette.

ROTHKO: *(Seriously.)* These young artists are out to murder me.

KEN: That's kind of extreme.

ROTHKO: But not inaccurate.

KEN: You think Jasper Johns is trying to murder you?

ROTHKO: Yes.

Beat.

KEN: What about Frank Stella?

ROTHKO: Yes.

KEN: Robert Rauschenberg?

ROTHKO: Yes.

KEN: Roy Lichtenstein?

ROTHKO: Which one is he?

KEN: Comic books.

ROTHKO: Yes.

Beat. Then the coup de grace:

KEN: Andy Warhol?

ROTHKO doesn't even answer.

KEN: You sound like an old man.

ROTHKO: I am an old man.

KEN: Not that old.

ROTHKO: Today, I'm old.

KEN: If you say so.

KEN goes back to working on the stretcher.

ROTHKO gets a Scotch.

ROTHKO: My point is… People like me… My contemporaries, my colleagues… Those painters who came up with me. We all had one thing in common… We understood the importance of seriousness.

Beat.

KEN: You're too much.

ROTHKO: What?

KEN: You heard me.

ROTHKO turns and really looks at him.

This challenging tone is new from KEN.

ROTHKO: What did you say to me?

KEN: Who are you to assume they're not serious?

ROTHKO: Look at their work.

KEN: I have.

ROTHKO: Not like you usually look at things, like an overeager undergraduate –

KEN: *I have.*

ROTHKO: Then what do you see?

KEN: Never mind.

ROTHKO: No. You look at them, what do you see?

KEN: This moment, right now.

ROTHKO: In all those flags and comic books and soup cans?

KEN: This moment, right now, and a little bit tomorrow.

ROTHKO: And you think that's good?

KEN: It's neither good nor bad, but it's what people want.

ROTHKO: Exactly my point.

KEN: So art shouldn't be popular at all now?

ROTHKO: It shouldn't *only* be popular.

KEN: You may not like it, but nowadays as many people are genuinely moved by Frank Stella as by Mark Rothko.

ROTHKO: That's nonsense.

KEN: Don't think so.

ROTHKO: You know the problem with those painters? It's *exactly* what you said: they are painting for this moment right now. And that's all. It's nothing but zeitgeist art. Completely temporal, completely disposable, like Kleenex, like –

KEN: Like Campbell's soup, like comic books –

ROTHKO: You really think Andy Warhol will be hanging in museums in a hundred years? Alongside the Bruegels and the Vermeers?

KEN: He's hanging alongside Rothko now.

ROTHKO: Because those goddamn galleries will do anything for money – cater to any wicked taste. That's *business*, young man, not art!

KEN approaches. Not backing down.

KEN: You ever get tired of telling people what art is?

ROTHKO: No, not ever. Until they listen. Better you should tell me? Fuck off.

KEN: You're just mad because the Barbarians are at the gate. And, whattaya know, people seem to like the Barbarians.

ROTHKO: Of course they *like* them. That's the goddamn point! You know what people *like*? Happy, bright colors. They want things to be *pretty*. They want things to be *beautiful* – Jesus Christ, when someone tells me one of my pictures is 'beautiful' I want to vomit!

KEN: What's wrong with –?

ROTHKO: *(Explodes.)* 'Pretty.' 'Beautiful.' 'Nice.' '*Fine*.' That's our life now! Everything's 'fine.' We put on the funny nose and glasses and slip on the banana peel and the TV makes everything happy and everyone's laughing all the time, it's all so goddamn funny, it's our constitutional right to be amused all the time, isn't it? We're a smirking nation, living under the tyranny of 'fine.' How are you? Fine. How was your day? Fine. How are you feeling? Fine. How did you like the painting? Fine. Want some dinner? Fine… Well, let me tell you, *everything is not fine*!

He spins to his paintings.

ROTHKO: HOW ARE YOU?!… HOW WAS YOUR DAY?!… HOW ARE YOU FEELING? Conflicted. Nuanced. Troubled. Diseased. Doomed. I am not fine. We are not fine. We are anything but fine… Look at these pictures. *Look at them*! You see the dark rectangle, like a doorway, an aperture, yes, but it's also a gaping mouth letting out a silent howl of something feral and foul and primal and REAL. Not nice. Not fine. *Real.* A moan of rapture. Something divine or damned. Something immortal, not comic books or soup cans, something beyond me and beyond now. And whatever it is, it's not pretty and it's not fine… *(He grabs KEN's heart.)* … I AM HERE TO STOP YOUR HEART, YOU UNDERSTAND THAT?!… *(He slaps KEN's forehead.)* – I AM HERE TO MAKE YOU THINK!… I AM NOT HERE TO MAKE PRETTY PICTURES!

A long beat.

ROTHKO roams, disturbed, trying to recover his equilibrium.

KEN hasn't moved.

KEN: So said the Cubist, the second before you stomped him to death.

ROTHKO stops, looks at him.

KEN: 'Tragic, really, to grow superfluous in your own lifetime'… Right?… 'The child must banish the father. Respect him, but kill him'… Isn't that what you said?… You guys went after the Cubists and Surrealists and, boy, did you love it. And now your time has come and you don't want to go. Well, exit stage left, Rothko. Because Pop Art has banished Abstract Expressionism… I only pray to

God they have more generosity of spirit than you do, and allow you some dignity as you go.

He glances around at the paintings.

KEN: Consider: The last gasp of a dying race… Futility.

Beat.

KEN: Don't worry; you can always sign menus for money.

ROTHKO: How dare you?

KEN: Do you know where I live?

ROTHKO: *(Confused.)* What?

KEN: Do you know where I live in the city?

ROTHKO: No…

KEN: Uptown? Downtown? Brooklyn?

ROTHKO: No.

KEN: You know if I'm married?

ROTHKO: What?

KEN: You know if I'm married? Dating? Queer? Anything?

ROTHKO: No. Why should −?

KEN: *Two years* I've been working here. Eight hours a day, five days a week and you know nothing about me. You ever once asked me to dinner? Maybe come to your house?

ROTHKO: What is −?

KEN: You know I'm a painter, don't you?

ROTHKO: I suppose.

KEN: No, answer me, you know I'm a painter?

ROTHKO: Yes.

KEN: Have you ever once asked to look at my work?

ROTHKO: Why should I?

KEN: Why should you?

ROTHKO: You're an *employee.* This is about me. Everything here is about me. You don't like that; leave… Is that what this is all about? Baby feels wounded Daddy didn't pat him on the head? Mommy didn't hug you today?

KEN: Stop it –

ROTHKO: Don't blame me, I didn't kill them.

KEN: Stop it –!

ROTHKO: Go find a psychiatrist and quit whining to me about it, your neediness bores me –

KEN: *(Explodes.)* Bores you?! *Bores you*?! – Christ almighty, try working for *you* for a living! – The talking-talking-talking-jesus-christ-won't-he-ever-shut-up titanic self-absorption of the man! You stand there trying to look so deep when you're nothing but a solipsistic bully with your grandiose self-importance and lectures and arias and let's-look-at-the-fucking-canvas-for-another-few-weeks-let's-not-fucking-paint-let's-just-look. And the *pretension*! Jesus Christ, the *pretension*! I can't imagine any other painter in the history of art ever tried so hard to be SIGNIFICANT!

KEN roams angrily.

KEN: You know, not everything has to be so goddamn IMPORTANT all the time! Not every painting has to rip your guts out and expose your soul! Not everyone wants art that actually HURTS! Sometimes you just want a fucking still life or landscape or soup can or comic book! Which you might learn if you ever actually left your goddamn hermetically sealed *submarine* here with all the windows closed and no natural light – BECAUSE NATURAL LIGHT ISN'T GOOD ENOUGH FOR YOU!

ROTHKO lights a cigarette. He continues to stare at KEN.

51

KEN: But then *nothing* is ever good enough for you! Not even the people who buy your pictures! Museums are nothing but mausoleums, galleries are run by pimps and swindlers, and art collectors are nothing but shallow social-climbers. So who *is* good enough to own your art?! Anyone?!

He stops, slows, realizing.

KEN: Or maybe the real question is: who's good enough to even *see* your art?… Is it just possible *no one* is worthy to look at your paintings?… That's it, isn't it?… We have all been 'weighed in the balance and have been found wanting.'

He approaches ROTHKO.

KEN: You say you spend your life in search of real 'human beings,' people who can look at your pictures with compassion. But in your heart you no longer believe those people exist… So you lose faith… So you lose hope… So black swallows red.

Beat.

KEN is standing right before ROTHKO.

KEN: My friend, I don't think you'd recognize a real human being if he were standing right in front of you.

Pause.

ROTHKO's stern and uncompromising Old Testament glare makes KEN uneasy.

KEN's resolve starts to crumble.

He moves away.

KEN: Never mind.

ROTHKO: Don't give up so easy!

KEN: It's not a game.

ROTHKO: You do make one salient point, though not the one you think.

KEN: Naturally.

ROTHKO: I do get depressed when I think how people are going to see my pictures. If they're going to be unkind… Selling a picture is like sending a blind child into a room full of razor blades. It's going to get hurt and it's never been hurt before, it doesn't know what hurt is.

He looks around at the mural paintings.

ROTHKO: That's why I'm looking to do something different with these ones. They're less vulnerable somehow, more robust, some hues from the earth even to give them strength. And they're not *alone*. They're a series, they'll always have each other for companionship and protection… And most important they're going into a *place* created just for them. A place of reflection and safety…

KEN: A place of contemplation…

ROTHKO: Yes…

KEN: A place with no distractions…

ROTHKO: Yes…

KEN: A sacred space…

ROTHKO: Yes…

KEN: A chapel…

ROTHKO: Yes…

KEN: Like the Four Seasons restaurant.

ROTHKO stops.

KEN shakes his head.

KEN: At least Andy Warhol gets the joke.

ROTHKO: No, you don't understand –

KEN: It's a fancy restaurant in a big high rise owned by a rich corporation, what don't I understand?

ROTHKO: You don't understand my intention –

KEN: Your intention is immaterial. Unless you're going to stand there for the rest of your life next to the pictures giving lectures – which you'd probably enjoy. The art has to speak for itself, yes?

ROTHKO: Yes, but –

KEN: Just admit your hypocrisy: the High Priest of Modern Art is painting a wall in the Temple of Consumption. You rail against commercialism in art, but pal, you're taking the money.

ROTHKO: I –

KEN: Sure, you can try to kid yourself you're making a holy place of contemplative awe, but in reality you're just decorating another dining room for the super-rich and these things – *(He gestures to the murals.)* – are nothing but the world's most expensive *overmantles*.

The words sting ROTHKO.

Beat.

ROTHKO: Why do you think I took this commission?

KEN: It appealed to your vanity.

ROTHKO: How so?

KEN: They could have gone to de Kooning, they went to you… It's the flashiest mural commission since the Sistine Chapel.

ROTHKO: You would have turned it down?

KEN: In a second.

ROTHKO: Easy for you to say.

KEN: You know what it is? It's your Oldsmobile convertible... Come on, you don't need the money. You don't need the publicity. Why make yourself a hypocrite for the Seagram Corporation?

ROTHKO: I didn't enter into this capriciously, you know. I *thought* about it.

KEN: No kidding.

ROTHKO: And of course it appealed to my vanity, I'm a human being too. But still I hesitated... The very same thoughts: is it corrupt? is it immoral? just feeding the whims of the bourgeoisie? should I do it?... I'm still thinking what the murals might look like when I take a trip to Europe. I happened to go to Michelangelo's Medici Library in Florence. You been there?

KEN: No.

ROTHKO: When you go, be sure to find the staircase, it's hidden away. It's a tiny vestibule, like a vault it's so cramped, but it goes up for three stories. Michelangelo embraced this claustrophobia and created false doors and windows all the way up the walls, rectangles in rich reds and browns... Well, that was it... He achieved just the kind of feeling I was after for the Four Seasons. He makes the viewer feel he is trapped in a room where all the doors and windows are bricked up, so all he can do is butt his head against the wall forever.

He turns to KEN:

ROTHKO: I know that place is where the richest bastards in New York will come to feed and show off... And I hope to ruin the appetite of every son-of-a-bitch who eats there.

KEN: You mention this to the Seagram's people?

ROTHKO: It would be a compliment if they turned the murals down. They won't.

KEN thinks about this.

Beat.

ROTHKO: You wanna drink?

KEN: *(Surprised.)* Sure.

ROTHKO pours two glasses of Scotch. He gives one to KEN.

Beat.

KEN: I don't know…

ROTHKO: What?

KEN: I don't know that I believe you.

ROTHKO: About what?

KEN: *(Referring to the murals.)* Them – This malicious intent of yours. The old lion still roaring, still trying to provoke, to be relevant, stick it to the bourgeoisie – it doesn't scan.

ROTHKO: Too romantic for you?

KEN: Too cruel to them. Your paintings aren't weapons. You would never do that to them, never reduce them like that. Maybe you started the commission thinking that way but… then art happened… You couldn't help it, that's what you do. So now you're stuck. You've painted yourself into a corner, you should forgive the expression.

KEN moves away.

ROTHKO remains standing, unsure.

ROTHKO: No, you're wrong.

KEN doesn't respond.

ROTHKO: Their power will transcend the setting. Working together, moving in rhythm, whispering to each other, they will still create a *place.*

His words sound hollow.

ROTHKO: You think I'm kidding myself.

KEN doesn't answer.

ROTHKO: You think it's all an act of monumental self-delusion… Answer me.

ROTHKO stares at KEN.

ROTHKO: Answer me.

KEN: Yes.

ROTHKO continues to stare intensely at KEN.

Beat.

KEN: I'm fired, aren't I?

ROTHKO: Fired?… This is the first time you've existed.

ROTHKO drains his Scotch, takes his hat and overcoat.

ROTHKO: See you tomorrow.

He goes.

A beat as KEN stands, a little mystified.

Then he moves forward to study the central painting.

He stands, glass of Scotch in one hand, tilting his head, very Rothko-like.

SCENE FIVE

The room is almost in darkness.

Classical music plays loudly from the phonograph.

ROTHKO is slumped awkwardly on the floor, gazing up at the central picture.

There is a bottle of Scotch and a bucket of red paint next to him. He has been drinking for a long time, but is not drunk. He can barely be seen in the gloom.

A long beat.

KEN enters.

KEN: *(Over the music.)* CAN I LOWER THE MUSIC?

ROTHKO doesn't respond. KEN lowers the volume.

Then he turns on some more lights:

He stops –

It is a shocking sight –

ROTHKO's hands and arms are dripping with red.

It's paint, but looks just like blood.

KEN thinks he has slashed his wrists.

KEN: Jesus Christ –!

He hurries to ROTHKO, panicked.

KEN: What did you do?!… *(Realizes it is paint.)* … Oh Christ, it's paint!

ROTHKO: I was going to work.

KEN: Obviously… Jesus Christ… You want a towel or something? Maybe a paint brush?

KEN gets a bucket of water. He cleans ROTHKO's hands.

Beat.

ROTHKO: I went there.

KEN: What?

ROTHKO: The Four Seasons.

KEN: Ah.

ROTHKO: After our 'chat' yesterday… I went there last night. For dinner.

KEN: Ah.

ROTHKO: It's been open a couple weeks now, thought I should finally take a look…

KEN: And…?

ROTHKO pulls himself up.

He stands there, unsteady. Stares forward, lost in thought.

Beat.

KEN: What do you see?

ROTHKO shakes his head.

KEN: What do you see?

Beat.

ROTHKO: *(Reliving it.)* You go in from 52nd… Then you go up some stairs to the restaurant… You *hear* the room before you see it. Glasses clinking, silverware, voices, hushed here but building as you get closer, it's a desperate sound, like forced gaiety at gunpoint… You go in, feel underdressed, feel fat, feel too goddamn Jewish for this place. Give your name. Pretty hostess gives you a look that says: 'I know who you are and I'm not impressed, we get millionaires in here, pal, for all I care you might as well be some schmuck painting marionettes in Tijuana.' She snaps for the Maitre D' who snaps for the captain who snaps for the head waiter who brings you through the crowd to your table, heads turning, everyone looking at everyone else all the time, like predators – who are you? what are you worth? do I need to fear you? do I need to acquire you?… Wine guy comes, speaks French, you feel inadequate, you obviously don't understand, he doesn't care. You embarrass yourself ordering something expensive to impress the wine guy. He goes, unimpressed. You look around. Everyone else seems to belong here: men with elegant silver hair and women with capes and gloves. Someone else in a uniform brings you the menu. It's things you never heard of: suckling pig under glass, quail eggs in aspic. You are lost. And then…

you can't help it, you start hearing what people are saying around you… Which is the worst of all…

ROTHKO pulls himself up.

He stands there, unsteady. It's disquieting: the dripping red paint really does look like blood.

ROTHKO: The voices… It's the chatter of monkeys and the barking of jackals. It's not human… And everyone's clever and everyone's laughing and everyone's investing in this or that and everyone's on this charity board or that and everyone's jetting off here or there and no one looks at anything and no one thinks about anything and all they do is chatter and bark and eat and the knives and forks click and clack and the words cut and the teeth snap and snarl.

Beat.

He spreads his arms, taking in his murals:

ROTHKO: And in that place – *there* – will live my paintings for all time.

Beat.

He finally turns to KEN:

ROTHKO: I wonder… Do you think they'll ever forgive me?

KEN: They're only paintings.

KEN stares at him.

It's like a challenge.

ROTHKO holds his gaze.

Pause.

And then ROTHKO seems to come to some decision.

He gets angry.

He nods.

He goes to the cluttered counter and finds the phone. He looks up.

ROTHKO: *(Referring to the phonograph.)* Turn that off, would ya?

KEN turns off the record player as ROTHKO dials.

ROTHKO: *(On phone.)* Mister Philip Johnson, please. This is Mark Rothko on the line… *(he waits, then.)* … Philip, this is Rothko. Listen, I went to the restaurant last night and lemme tell you, anyone who eats that kind of food for that kind of money in that kind of joint will never look at a painting of mine. I'm sending the money back and I'm keeping the pictures. No offence. This is how it goes. Good luck to ya, buddy.

He hangs up with a joyous finality.

KEN: *(Proud.)* Now…now you are Mark Rothko.

ROTHKO: Only poorer.

KEN: Having money doesn't make you wealthy.

ROTHKO: It helps though.

KEN: Well, this is a day for the books, we'll have to –

ROTHKO: You're fired.

KEN stops.

KEN: What?

ROTHKO: You're fired.

Beat.

KEN stares at him. He can't believe it.

KEN: Why?

ROTHKO busies himself organizing something.

ROTHKO: Doesn't matter.

KEN: It does.

ROTHKO: Write down your address, I'll send your final check.

KEN: You owe me an explanation.

ROTHKO: I don't owe you anything –

KEN pursues. ROTHKO tries to avoid him. The conflict builds:

KEN: Two years and you expect me to walk out, just like that?

ROTHKO: You want a retirement party?

KEN: I want a reason.

ROTHKO: None of your business.

KEN: I want a reason.

ROTHKO: Look, you're too goddamn needy, all right? I don't need it. I don't need your need. Since you're seven you're looking for a home – well this isn't it, and I'm not your father. Your father's dead, remember? Sorry, but that's it.

KEN isn't deterred.

KEN: Come on, Doctor Freud. You can do better. *Why?*

ROTHKO: I told you.

KEN: Why?

ROTHKO: Because I don't need an assistant –

KEN: Bullshit.

ROTHKO: Because you talk too much –

KEN: So do you.

ROTHKO: Because you have lousy taste –

KEN: Bullshit.

ROTHKO: Because I'm sick of you –

KEN: Bullshit –

ROTHKO spins on him, points to the outside:

ROTHKO: *Because your life is out there!*

Beat.

ROTHKO: Listen, kid, you don't need to spend any more time with me. You need to find your contemporaries and make your own world, your own life… You need to get *out there* now, into the thick of it, shake your fist at them, talk their ear off…

ROTHKO steps close, touches KEN.

ROTHKO: *Make them look.*

KEN is moved.

ROTHKO continues with quiet emotion.

ROTHKO: When I was your age, art was a lonely thing: no galleries, no collecting, no critics, no money. We didn't have mentors. We didn't have parents. We were alone. But it was a great time, because we had nothing to lose and a vision to gain.

Beat.

ROTHKO: Okay?

KEN: Okay.

Beat.

KEN: Thank you.

ROTHKO: Make something new.

KEN gathers his things, starts to go.

He stops at the door.

He turns back. He takes in the paintings and ROTHKO one last time.

ROTHKO: *(Referring to the central painting.)* What do you see?

KEN looks at the painting.

But then he looks at ROTHKO.

Beat.

KEN: Red.

Beat.

KEN goes to the phonograph and puts on a record.

Classical music plays.

KEN goes.

ROTHKO seems a little lost.

He moves to the central painting and stares at it.

Pause.

ROTHKO stands alone.

The End.

PETER AND ALICE

Peter and Alice by John Logan was first performed in London on 9 March 2013 at the Noël Coward Theatre as part of the Michael Grandage Company Season of five plays, with the following cast and creative team:

Cast (in order of speaking)

PETER LLEWELYN DAVIES	Ben Whishaw
ALICE LIDDELL HARGREAVES	Dame Judi Dench
LEWIS CARROLL (REV. CHARLES DODGSON)	Nicholas Farrell
JAMES BARRIE	Derek Riddell
PETER PAN	Olly Alexander
ALICE IN WONDERLAND	Ruby Bentall
ARTHUR DAVIES/REGINALD (REGGIE) HARGREAVES/ MICHAEL DAVIES	Stefano Braschi

Understudies

ALICE IN WONDERLAND	Georgina Beedle
LEWIS CARROLL/JIM BARRIE	Henry Everett
PETER LLEWLYN DAVIES/ PETER PAN/ARTHUR DAVIES/ REGGIE HARGREAVES/ MICHAEL DAVIES	Christopher Leveaux
ALICE LIDDELL HARGREAVES	Pamela Merrick

Creative Team

Director	Michael Grandage
Set and Costume Designer	Christopher Oram
Lighting Designer	Paule Constable
Composer and Sound Designer	Adam Cork

Note

Many years ago I came across the following in *The Real Alice*, Anne Clark's biography of Alice Liddell Hargreaves, the model for Lewis Carroll's Alice in Wonderland:

"*On June 26 1932, Alice opened the Lewis Carroll exhibition at Bumpus, the London bookshop. Beside her was Peter Davies, the original Peter Pan.*"

I wondered what they said to each other.

Characters

in order of appearance:

PETER LLEWELYN DAVIES

ALICE LIDDELL HARGREAVES

LEWIS CARROLL (REV. CHARLES DODGSON)

JAMES BARRIE

PETER PAN

ALICE IN WONDERLAND

ARTHUR DAVIES

REGINALD (REGGIE) HARGREAVES

MICHAEL DAVIES

*(Arthur Davies, Reginald Hargreaves and Michael Davies
may be played by the same actor.)*

Setting

The backroom of the Bumpus bookshop.

No. 350, Oxford Street. London.

June 26, 1932.

And corners of memory that include Oxford, a riverbank, a street with illuminations, a darkroom, a country estate, a London flat, Neverland and Wonderland, variously from 1862 to 1921.

Quotes from the novels *Peter and Wendy* by J.M. Barrie and *Alice's Adventures in Wonderland* and *Through the Looking-Glass* by Lewis Carroll are in *italics*... These novels are in the public domain.

Dedicated to Michael Grandage
for his faith in this play and its author.
And for giving an actor the single best piece
of direction I have ever heard.

The backroom of the Bumpus bookshop in London. June 26, 1932.

Imposing shelves of books, files, bibliographic supplies, etc. There is a door into the bookshop.

PETER waits. He's in his 30s.

He hears voices off. He prepares himself, clears his throat, and straightens his conservative suit. He's nervous.

ALICE enters.

She's 80.

PETER: Mrs. Hargreaves… My name is Peter Davies. How do you do?

ALICE: How do you do?

PETER: We're to wait here. I'm told.

Beat.

PETER: It'll only be a few minutes, until everyone has gathered and then Charles will introduce me and I'll introduce you. You're to make some remarks and then–

ALICE: I understand.

Beat.

PETER: This is a – pleasure, ma'am.

ALICE: You were going to say "honor" but you thought it unduly reverential. It is challenging to know which note to strike with me. Do you honor him and the book through honoring me? But am I worthy of honor? Not her – me… Then how, indeed, do I feel about her? You've no way of knowing… Is it an "honor" or a "pleasure"…or something else altogether?

PETER: I think, now, the latter.

She smiles slightly.

He's emboldened to continue.

PETER: In any event, Mrs. Hargreaves, I've been looking forward to meeting you.

ALICE: No, Mr. Davies, I daresay you've been looking forward to meeting <u>her</u>.

PETER: It is to <u>you</u> I wish to speak.

ALICE: Is this by way of an ambush?

PETER: I asked Charles if I might have a few words with you.

She nods. Proceed.

PETER: I have an imprint, not inconsiderable, called Peter Davies Limited. We have a proper list and my chief duty as publisher is to cast my eye about for worthwhile subjects.

ALICE: And your eye has fallen on me, as worthwhile. How very flattering.

PETER: That's the curse of my trade. To a book man, every nook and cranny is a potential story.

ALICE: Am I a nook or a cranny?

PETER: I – Sorry?

ALICE: Come to the point, Mr. Davies.

PETER: When I got the invitation to come and meet you, I thought: there's a story, and worth the telling… Have you considered your memoirs?

ALICE: Considered them as what?

PETER: Something you might wish to write.

ALICE: To be published and vended?

PETER: Yes.

ALICE: This is not the first time I've been approached.

PETER: Perhaps never by someone with such a <u>personal</u> understanding of your unique position.

ALICE: Have I a "position"?

PETER: Come now, Mrs. Hargreaves, you would not be here today if you did not.

She grants the point.

ALICE: Memoirs – autobiographies – are the records of the deeds of a life. I have had no deeds worthy of reportage. Not of my own... Those around me perhaps.

PETER: Isn't every life worth recording honestly?

ALICE: Oh... You want <u>honesty</u>.

Beat.

ALICE: Aren't you the ambitious young man?

She strolls, considers the room.

ALICE: In your element, Mr. Davies.

PETER: Sorry?

ALICE: Amongst the books.

PETER: For you as well.

ALICE: I was not amongst the books, I was <u>in</u> a book. That's something different.

She runs her hand along some of the spines.

ALICE: From the outside they are one thing: ordered and symmetrical, all the same; like foot soldiers. From the inside they are altogether singular.

PETER: Do you ever get tired of it?

ALICE: What?

PETER: Being Alice.

ALICE: I'm loath to disillusion you, but people have forgotten me. Thus I fear for the commercial prospects of the House of Davies should you be so reckless as to publish my memoirs. Of course they remember <u>her</u>. But <u>me</u>? ... Those days are like the dark ages now, aren't they? Before motor cars and chewing gum. Before airplanes and cinema and the wireless. Lord, a time before the <u>wireless</u>, can you imagine the silence? You could hear the bees buzzing in the summer... Golden afternoons all gone away.

PETER: With respect, Mrs. Hargreaves, people have not forgotten. Everything associated with the Centenary is taking the fancy of the nation, including the reception today.

ALICE: Momentarily, yes... But before this there was, and after this there shall be, quietude. I like to hear the bees buzzing.

PETER: But don't you think – ?

ALICE: *(Firm.)* No, sir, I do not. In your quest for literary "truth" you must occasionally run across those stories you wish you hadn't told, for the simple reason that no one really wants to hear the truth when it runs contrary – "contrariwise" as he would say – to the comfortable assumptions that people hold so dear. That's the burden of truth, isn't it?

PETER: Yes, but–

ALICE: Here's a burden: the only reason anyone remembers me now as Alice in Wonderland is that I decided to sell my hand-written manuscript of the book. It was this act that brought me back into the public eye... But do you know <u>why</u> I sold the manuscript? Because I needed the money. <u>To heat my house, Mr. Davies</u>... Now, is that the Alice people want to know? Or is it just possible they would rather remember that little blond girl in the dress, eternally inquisitive, impossibly bold, never changing and never growing old?

PETER: <u>But we all grow old!</u> ... That's the story of our lives: the one immutable; the one inescapable. The crocodile in the lagoon, the iceberg on the horizon, death just around the corner, tick tick tick. I'm grasping now but–

ALICE: *(Interrupts.)* <u>What's your name</u>?

PETER: Peter Davies, ma'am.

ALICE: All of it.

PETER: Peter Llewelyn Davies.

ALICE: Peter Pan.

Beat.

PETER: There were five of us.

ALICE: Well, this is rich!

PETER: I suppose so.

ALICE: And a little bizarre.

PETER: Mm.

ALICE: Were you planning on telling me?

PETER: No, actually, I wasn't intending –

ALICE: Of course not. But how could you help being who you are?

PETER: And how can you?

It's a bit of a challenge.

She moves around the room.

ALICE: Alice in Wonderland and Peter Pan. We're practically our own children's book department... There were five of you?

PETER: Five boys, yes. Five brothers... And there were three sisters?

ALICE: Yes, we three Liddell girls, back in Oxford.

PETER: But you're "Alice."

ALICE: As you're "Peter"... But after all, what's in a name?

PETER: What isn't?

She understands.

ALICE: With me, it has been a wholly happy connection. When people find out, they always smile, for they're bringing so many associations with them: first time hearing the story; first time reading the book; then reading it to their own children. You see it in their faces, the pictures behind that smile of recognition: the White Rabbit; the Mad Hatter; the Cheshire Cat. I think they smile because what they're really remembering is <u>themselves as children</u>, and for that moment I see the wonder returning to them... When I look over my days I feel I was given a gift by Mr. Dodgson. Out of everyone, there's only one Alice. He made me <u>special</u>. And that uniqueness has given me a lifetime of people looking back at me, with a growing smile, remembering their better selves, when they were new and life was before them and all they needed to find their way through was a little courage, a little imagination, and a bottle labeled "Drink Me."

PETER: I heard that speech on the wireless a few weeks ago.

ALICE: Well it is my speech.

PETER: Very effective.

ALICE: I'm glad you think so. You'll be hearing it again in a few minutes.

PETER: Lovely words. But we know better though.

ALICE: Do we?

PETER: I think so.

ALICE: You're presumptuous.

PETER: The truth isn't so easy.

ALICE: Ah, there's the "truth" again.

PETER: Let me tell you the rest of the story and you tell me... So, yes, the smile of recognition, all the associations coming back: the first time they saw the play; the first time they read the book. Peter and Wendy. Neverland. Captain Hook. Tinkerbell... But a second after those happy memories comes that look of confusion and doubt, and then this in their eyes: "But how can you be Peter Pan?

You? The Boy Who Never Grew Up? That's not you. You have egg on your collar. You can't fly. You're not Alice. Alice was a little blond girl, I know she was. You're lying to me." <u>And then they remember</u>. <u>What growing up really is</u>: when they learned that boys can't fly and mermaids don't exist and White Rabbits don't talk and all boys grow old, even Peter Pan, as you've grown old. They've been <u>deceived</u>. As if you've somehow been lying to them. So following hard on the smile of remembrance is the pain in the eyes, which you've caused, every time you meet someone.

ALICE: How can you say it's a lie? They're just stories.

PETER: As a publisher I've an obligation to tell the truth.

ALICE: You talk like a very young man, and callow. The truth isn't a mathematical equation that always works out to the precise sum. It's variable. It's mutable. Lord, the longer I live the more I know there's no such thing as <u>certainty</u>! There are only passing moments, and I savor the ones that bring me some damn comfort in a cold house. If it's a lie, why does it keep me warm?

PETER: It doesn't and it can't.

ALICE: You're presumptuous again.

PETER: I'm sorry.

ALICE: You're not at all. You think you're being clever: "No one gets the better of me. I see the world as it really is. I'm a marvelous honest fellow. Pity the poor old lady living in her memories of things that never happened." You're so young. You are the Boy Who Never Grew Up!

PETER: Believe me; the one thing I thoroughly know is <u>growing up</u>!

ALICE: Then tell me.

PETER: What?

ALICE: What is "growing up" precisely?

PETER: Well, I suppose…

ALICE: Specifically.

PETER: I don't know that I can –

ALICE: It's the one thing you "thoroughly know."

PETER: Well, it's <u>complicated</u> –

ALICE: Is it?

PETER: I wouldn't know where to start –

ALICE: Was it the day you realized your parents aren't perfect? When you got your first long trousers? Going to school? Saying hello? Saying goodbye? Your heart opens? It breaks? It heals? It breaks again? Which is it?

PETER: When you realize what life is.

ALICE: Too vague. You're after the <u>truth</u>, aren't you? Being a publisher and all?

He looks at her. She is like iron staring back at him.

He reorients himself in the room.

PETER: Do you think back on your life?

ALICE: As rarely as possible.

PETER: Will you try?

ALICE: Why should I?

PETER: To help me understand. We can swap a truth for a truth.

ALICE: I'm not sure I trust you…

PETER: Who but me? Peter and Alice.

Suddenly, a man's voice is heard:

CARROLL: *(Offstage.)* <u>Alice</u>! … <u>Alice</u>! Where have you gone?

ALICE is utterly shocked at this voice from her past.

CARROLL: *(Offstage.)* Are you hiding, Queen Alice?

PETER: Yes, of course that's how it begins: a harmless fairy tale to pass the hours…

The bookstore disappears around ALICE and PETER.

We're in their minds and memories now.

LEWIS CARROLL sidles up to ALICE. He's slanted, awkward, partly deaf and painfully shy.

CARROLL: I can't do it without you, my lady. What am I without you? But then, <u>what are you without me</u>? … Take my hand.

He offers his hand.

CARROLL: Be young again.

PETER: Who wouldn't want that?

CARROLL: Be young forever.

PETER: He offers your heart's desire.

ALICE: Stop the clocks. Turn down the lights. In the glass, the wrinkles fade away. The skin is fresh again. The bones don't ache. To be always poised on the verge of the great adventure. Everything <u>just ahead</u>.

CARROLL: Take my hand, little Alice.

PETER: But there's a price. He feeds on your youth.

ALICE: Or do I feed on his experience?

This stops PETER.

She looks deeply at CARROLL.

ALICE: Are we to have a story on the river?

CARROLL: We shall have whatever you like.

ALICE: Please then, Reverend Dodgson, <u>a story</u>.

She takes his hand.

PETER: And it's done… That first touch.

ALICE: His skin is soft! Like a pampered man who never uses his hands. It's repulsive… But it didn't feel so then.

PETER: Your hand was less used to other hands then.

CARROLL strolls with her.

It's a hot summer day, the lovely buzz of insects. It is 1862.

CARROLL: Well, first things being first: if we're to have a story then we must have a p-p-p–

The word doesn't come. His mouth gapes horribly.

This is his stammer.

He starts to panic.

CARROLL: P-p-p-p…

ALICE: Pirate? Poetess?

PETER: Protagonist?

CARROLL: P-p-protagonist. Who shall be our heroine? Shall it be one of your sisters? Shall it be Lorina? Or shall it be Edith?

ALICE: Me!

CARROLL: Why you then, Alice?

ALICE: Because I am your dream child. Because they're awfully silly and I'm not. We understand each other, Mr. Dodgson.

CARROLL: Like two cryptographers, unlocking the same secret.

ALICE: I don't know that word.

CARROLL: That's a word you learn when you're eleven, along with crepuscular and cantilevered… So if we can't be cryptographers, perhaps we'd best be polar explorers, roped together lest a crevasse or snow-blindness make us lose our way.

ALICE: I don't see how one can become blind in snow. I could see losing your way in a cave, or at the bottom of the sea.

PETER: Or in memory.

CARROLL: I wonder if we'll lose our way someday, Alice?

ALICE: I would think that depends on where we're going in the first place.

PETER: You weren't that clever.

ALICE: I am now.

CARROLL: It's a simple thing to get lost, you know. You glance around and suddenly everything's changed. Nothing's like it was, even you in the looking glass. Who you thought you were, you're not… And you don't need to be exploring another c-c-c-continent either. You can lose your way right here in Oxford if you're not careful. Right over that hedge.

ALICE: Or down that rabbit hole.

PETER: You didn't bait him like that.

CARROLL tells a story. He's enchanting.

The buzzing of the insects becomes intoxicating music.

CARROLL: So imagine a day like this and a girl like you and a sister like Lorina and you find yourself on a riverbank, and there's a rabbit hole nearby, and perhaps you had one too many jam tarts this morning, so you're ever so soporific, which is a twelve-year-old word in truth, so on this particular, peculiar day you fall asleep…

CARROLL continues quietly.

ALICE: The maladroit stutter, the slanting body, the dreadful shyness all disappeared that afternoon, that golden afternoon when I was ten and we went up the river with my sisters, and we were in the shadow of a haycock because it was blazing hot, and he told the story of Alice underground, <u>my</u> story, which would have died like one of the summer midges, like all the others, only this time I asked him to write it down, because I was the heroine, that day he was <u>beautiful</u>.

Beat.

ALICE: That day he had all he needed… He had his story.

PETER: But what man can live on words?

ALICE: He was a writer.

PETER: He was a man.

ALICE: Not much of one.

He looks at her, the sharpness surprising.

She moves away from CARROLL. CARROLL remains. (Once characters are introduced they remain on stage. Lingering like memories or ghosts.)

ALICE: Not the way I've come to know men, adult men. He was a perpetual child.

PETER: There's no such thing.

ALICE: You didn't know him.

She moves away from him. He pursues.

PETER: Did you?

ALICE: For several years he was at the very center of our lives.

PETER: "The center of your lives?"

ALICE: Yes. He'd tell us his stories, on the green or rowing on the river, and then off he'd go to let us dream about them.

PETER: And where did he go?

ALICE: I beg your pardon?

PETER: When he left you, where did he go, what did he do?

ALICE: I don't know… I imagine he returned home and went on with his life.

PETER: No. He didn't. <u>You</u> were his life.

She stops.

PETER: It's just like Barrie with us… You weren't a "dream child." You were a child of flesh and bone. He looked into your eyes and you looked back.

ALICE: We were a diversion, no more. He was a grown man with an important career and friends of his own… Three adolescent girls, all giggles and elbows? I'm sure he was happy to go home and forget us.

PETER: <u>Grown men do not "return home and go on with their lives.</u>" That's what children do. Children pass gaily through life with no sense of the weight of events… Grown ups look in the mirror, and then look at the clock… They walk into an empty house that feels emptier every day that passes, for it brings them ever-closer to the final and inescapable loneliness: that last echoing room where you are truly alone.

Beat.

PETER: There are no simple childhood memories, Mrs. Hargreaves. I told you, it's complicated. Everything's occluded.

ALICE: How do you know he was lonely?

PETER: Ah… If he were not, would he have loved you so much?

ALICE: How do you know he loved me?

PETER: Would he have written the book otherwise?

ALICE: So…it's to be a love story.

PETER: Aren't they all?

A voice surprises him:

BARRIE: *(Offstage.)* No, Peter, you're wrong… There's no <u>love</u> in it! No romance, I promise you that…

JAMES BARRIE enters briskly and goes toward PETER. He's a stunted, sad, inspiring Scotsman.

BARRIE: There's not a jot of love or moonlight to be had, except for that moon which can be glimpsed at dead midnight over the Tyburn gallows after those bloodthirsty brigands have met their end and sway from the gibbet. Gather 'round, lads…

He continues his story. It is 1901.

Music builds.

BARRIE: Here at Black Lake Cottage there's a lake which – you will not be surprised to learn – is black. But do you know <u>why</u> it's black? Not the murky water, though tolerably murky it is. Not the depth of it where no light can pass, though deep it is. It's black because of the souls of all the dead men trapped at the bottom, it's been blackened by wickedness, by them that walked the plank, that felt the touch o' the cat, that had their throats slit by that fearsome captain afore his breakfast. What's his name again?

PETER: I can't remember…

ALICE: You mean you can't forget.

BARRIE: What's his name again, Peter?

PETER: Really, I don't –

ALICE: You do.

BARRIE: Come on now! … Feel the spray of the ocean, like you used to when you were a boy; when you wanted to sail the seas on a triple-master, like every boy does, to see the world, to have adventures, to fly and fight and fly again.

CARROLL: Be young forever.

BARRIE: What's his name, that piratical gentleman who had us quaking under the covers at night?!

PETER: <u>Hook</u>!

BARRIE: Yes, Hook! Now you're with me! You're on the deck of the mighty galleon as it rolls and pitches, and we're lashed to the wheel together, lad, through the cataracts!

PETER: 'Round the Horn!

BARRIE: Until the maelstrom passes!

ALICE: Do you feel your heart pounding?!

PETER: Yes! Like racing passion, like love!

ALICE: So in a flash you're young again!

PETER tears himself away. The music fades.

ALICE: Can't help yourself.

PETER: You get caught up.

ALICE: I know.

PETER: You can't breathe.

ALICE: You don't want to.

PETER: That's their power, these writers, these men of words. Trap baited and sprung, and before you know it you have to chew your leg off to get free.

ALICE considers BARRIE.

ALICE: In truth he was a little man.

PETER: Not when he told his stories.

ALICE: Who's the romantic now? … I met him at a reception once and was surprised to find him so terribly diminutive. Famous people should not be so tiny, it seems dishonest.

PETER: From the first day, he was all words. My brothers and I were playing in the park and the most enormous dog came bounding over. His dog, Porthos, like a lure it was.

ALICE: There's that trap again.

PETER: How he enmeshed himself in our lives! Before long he was following us home and staying for supper, seemed to think it was his right. He just…acquired us… My father was so uncomfortable with him, fully aware he was being supplanted, but what was he to do? My mother loved him, as did we boys… Snap. The trap was sprung.

He looks at BARRIE.

PETER: You plain mesmerized us.

BARRIE: I made you famous.

PETER: I didn't ask for it.

ALICE: Didn't you?

PETER: For god's sake, I was a child. I didn't know anything!

ALICE: You listened. You laughed. You sparkled for him. You wanted him to look at you most, to look at you longest. To love you best.

CARROLL: You're my favorite, Alice. You'll always be my favorite.

ALICE: Your brothers were <u>rivals</u>.

PETER: Were your sisters?

ALICE: Yes.

PETER: It wasn't that way with us. We were a band of brothers.

BARRIE: My Lost Boys.

ALICE: I can see the five of you, each craning over the other, crawling over his lap like puppies. Whose eye will he catch? Who'll make him smile today?

PETER: <u>Michael</u>.

ALICE: What?

PETER: He loved Michael most… Uncle Jim always said that he made Peter Pan by rubbing the five of us violently together, as savages with two sticks produce a flame. But that's not true. It was Michael, bold and fearless Michael… I was never bold. I always had fear.

ALICE: Of what?

PETER: What does every child fear? … Captain Hook.

ALICE: The character?

PETER: The idea. Means something different for every boy I expect… For me it was no more summers of pirate yarns and playing in the grass. All the boys going to school, moving away and getting separated. My brothers not being my brothers anymore, being someone else's husband or father, but not my brothers, not really, not like it was. No more father and mother… Just me… That's a piece of growing up, isn't it? Learning to name the thing you fear? … Captain Hook.

CARROLL: Or the Red Queen.

ALICE: Children's stories can't hurt you.

PETER: You know better.

ALICE: They don't exist. There is no Captain Hook.

PETER: Are you sure? Don't you sometimes feel him? … When you're alone, in a dark room, the point of his hook touching the back of your neck?

ALICE: They can't hurt you. Not once you grow up.

CARROLL goes to her:

CARROLL: But, Alice, you must never grow up! <u>Promise me</u>!

ALICE: Really, how can I help from growing up?

CARROLL: Ah, the question of the ages. We'll have to ask a wise old tortoise. Shall we stroll?

She's disturbed by this bit of her past.

ALICE: That long summer. God, would it never end? … We were walking in town. There were illuminations that evening and the street was radiant. My sisters and our governess had wandered ahead, so it was just Reverend Dodgson and me… It was so rarely that, just the two of us alone. Only twice that I can recall.

PETER: Truly?

ALICE: It was a different era, Mr. Davies. Unaccompanied in the presence of a gentleman? It wasn't done… I can only remember two times. This was the first…

Gentle and magical illuminations light the stage.

CARROLL and ALICE stroll. It is 1862.

ALICE: But why mustn't I grow up? It seems the most marvelous thing in the world to be old and wear gowns and gloves and hats with feathers.

CARROLL: Oh, hats with feathers are admirable things, but along with them goes something altogether unlike gowns and gloves. First the squint in the eye and then the hard set of the mouth, followed in quick order by the wagging tongue and the shaking finger. One day you turn around and you've become Mrs. Grundy: soberly disapproving of everything that used to give you pleasure.

ALICE: I can't imagine that! Shan't I always be able to laugh at things?

CARROLL: Does your mother laugh much?

ALICE thinks about this.

ALICE: No… Not so much as she used to perhaps.

CARROLL: And it seems to me even our Lorina is not so amused as she used to be.

ALICE: She got her first corset, you know.

CARROLL: Alice, you shouldn't talk about such things to a gentleman.

ALICE: It's made out of whale bone!

CARROLL: That's why the leviathans are so terribly fat. They've given all their corsets to little girls in Oxford.

ALICE speaks to PETER:

ALICE: I watched my sister putting on her corset for the first time. I shall never forget it… My mother sat us down, all three girls, and produced it from a gorgeous purple box, made of Venetian paper I think. I was intoxicated by the box. And then the bone of the corset was <u>iridescent</u>. Here was growing up and becoming a woman: and it was <u>beautiful</u>… My mother helped Lorina put it on and tighten the laces. Well then I could see it hurt. Lorina cried… And my mother, the look on her face. She was not a woman given to displaying vulnerability. She was our soldier. But on her face… What was it? Not quite sadness. Acceptance. Resignation to something vast, and helpless to change it. Powerlessness… Here was growing up too.

CARROLL: We'll have to watch Lorina carefully, like a fever-sufferer, and at the first sign of the censorious eye, we'll strike.

ALICE: What'll we do?

CARROLL: Make her stand on her head.

ALICE is amused.

They walk for a moment.

CARROLL is thinking about something.

CARROLL: It's only a matter of the clock now. She'll be up and married and raising a litter of her own soon.

ALICE: Lorina?! She's still a baby.

CARROLL: She's thirteen. That's a whole year past the age of consent.

They walk for a beat.

CARROLL: Why, in two years <u>you</u> could get married.

There is weight to this.

ALICE: What was he trying to say?

PETER: You know exactly.

ALICE: <u>I was ten years old</u>.

PETER: You had fascinated him. Beaten out your sisters, like you said; your rivals. You sparkled for him. You got your wish.

ALICE: Stop it.

PETER: Don't you like love stories?

CARROLL: Alice, will you not look at me?

PETER: I thought all little girls enjoyed love stories.

ALICE: You're a terrible man.

PETER: And what kind of child were you?

ALICE: A child is what I was!

PETER: Not after that night. Might as well start chewing off your leg.

ALICE: You don't know anything about it! You didn't walk with him. You didn't feel his suffering. Like a vibration next to me, like a tuning fork, his need was overwhelming.

CARROLL: Alice? Please look at me.

ALICE pretends to peer ahead for her sisters.

ALICE: Where have they gone? Can you see my sisters? I should catch up with them.

CARROLL: Of course.

ALICE: All right. See you later, sir.

CARROLL: Alice – I've almost finished your story.

ALICE: You're writing it down, I'd forgotten. That's marvelous.

She moves off quickly.

CARROLL immediately stops walking. He stands alone.

ALICE recovers herself.

ALICE: What would I have done if I looked back and saw him standing there? Would my heart have broken?

PETER: Does it now?

ALICE: Children don't have hearts yet, not really. They haven't been hurt into the need for one... You know, Mr. Davies, I think they were born out of sadness, Alice and Peter. Out of <u>loneliness</u>, wouldn't you say?

PETER: Uncle Jim was the loneliest man I ever knew. For a time he could be a part of us, one of the boys, but that couldn't last because...

He stops, realizing where this has gone, inevitably...

PETER: *Because all children, except one, grow up...*

PETER PAN flies in. He's full of bravado and nerve and looks exactly as you imagine PETER PAN to look.

PETER PAN: *I ran away the day I was born! I heard father and mother talking about what I was to be when I became a man. I don't ever want to be a man. I always want to be a little boy and to have fun. So I ran away to Kensington Gardens and lived a long long time among the fairies.*

PETER: He created the one boy who would never grow up and leave him.

ALICE approaches PETER PAN:

ALICE: *Wendy felt at once that she was in the presence of a tragedy.*

PETER PAN: *Would you like an adventure now, or would you like to have your tea first?*

ALICE: *What kind of adventure?*

PETER PAN: *I'll teach you how to jump on the wind's back, and away we go!*

PETER: Away we go...

BARRIE: To fly and fight and fly again. Shall we do that, Peter?

PETER PAN: *How clever I am! Oh, the cleverness of me!*

CARROLL, who has not moved, looks up.

CARROLL: *Alice was beginning to get very tired of sitting by her sister on the bank, and of having nothing to do: once or twice she had*

*peeped into the book her sister was reading, but it had no pictures
or conversations in it...*

*ALICE IN WONDERLAND pops up from a trap door, like one of the
Tenniel illustrations come to life. She's a bold and curious girl.*

ALICE IN WONDERLAND: *And what's the use of a book without
pictures or conversations?!*

CARROLL: *So she was considering, in her own mind...*

ALICE IN WONDERLAND: *As well as she could, for the hot day
made her feel very sleepy and stupid...*

CARROLL: *Whether the pleasure of making a daisy-chain would be
worth the trouble of getting up and picking the daisies –*

ALICE IN WONDERLAND: *When suddenly a White Rabbit with
pink eyes ran close by her!*

PETER PAN and ALICE IN WONDERLAND linger nearby.

*They are curious about their real-life counterparts. They interact,
examine, imitate, and shadow them periodically throughout the play.*

ALICE: Once she was born, part of me ceased to exist. As if
she had taken part of me.

PETER: Or like a brother.

ALICE: Yes! Like I had another sister.

PETER: Another rival?

ALICE: No, a twin... A shadow.

PETER: That's it.

ALICE: Even when I had forgotten her for weeks on end, years
on end, I would turn, and even be a little surprised, for
there she was.

*PETER PAN shadows PETER, almost like a game for him. Not for
PETER though.*

PETER: Sometimes I tried to forget him. Always I tried to
forget him. It was unremitting my whole life: "Peter Pan
joins the Army", "Peter Pan marries", "Peter Pan opens

publishing firm" … There was a time I drank terribly to forget him. I still do, there's the truth. Or threw myself into love affairs, high drama, anything to forget the shadow. But, invariably, on the happiest of days, when he had been banished fully, I would catch a glimpse…in the shaving mirror…the shop window…behind me on the pavement.

ALICE: Why did you try to banish him?

He doesn't answer.

ALICE IN WONDERLAND: *Wendy had looked forward to thrilling talks with Peter about old times, but new adventures had crowded the old ones from his mind.*

PETER PAN: *Who's Captain Hook?*

ALICE IN WONDERLAND: *Don't you remember how you killed him and saved all our lives?!*

PETER PAN: *I forget them after I kill them.*

PETER: Because he makes me <u>remember</u>.

Beat.

This doesn't come easily.

PETER: When I look at my own children, Mrs. Hargreaves, I think…I think I know what childhood's for. It's to give us a bank of happy memories against future suffering. So when sadness comes, at least you can remember what it was to be happy.

ARTHUR LLEWELYN DAVIES, PETER's father, enters.

His neck and jaw are in a horrible leather brace. He is dying. It is 1907.

PETER: When it came, I was nine years old. Up until that time we were boys. After that time we were not.

ARTHUR sits painfully.

PETER PAN approaches, watches, almost impassive.

PETER: My father… It was a cancer of the jaw and mouth. The word was never spoken in our house. It was a filthy word… Well, the operations began for this thing we didn't say, and didn't end until they had removed half his upper jaw and his palate and his cheekbone. For a time he had an artificial jaw, which was monstrous, he was so disfigured. I couldn't look at him he frightened me so much, my father, more than Captain Hook, more than anything… He could barely speak. And every word had to be carefully chosen for the effort it cost him.

BARRIE sits with ARTHUR. He's very gentle with him.

PETER: Barrie was magnificent those last days. The best he ever was. So kind to him, to us all… He paid for everything, you see. My father had lost his job. No one wants a barrister who can't speak, who looks like that… There was no money and no prospects so in the end, my father was trapped…

BARRIE: Don't speak, Arthur. Let me tell you about the boys. George wrote to me from Eton that he wants to come for the weekend, but I wonder if –

ARTHUR: Jim.

BARRIE: Are you sure you should?

ARTHUR holds up a hand, he must try to speak.

This is agony:

ARTHUR: There is no money… There is my wife… There are five boys.

It is too hard to continue.

BARRIE: Shall I try to find the words for you?

ARTHUR nods.

BARRIE: You're thinking about them now, about the future. You wonder once you've gone what'll become of them.

ARTHUR nods.

BARRIE: You look at me and you feel apprehension.

ARTHUR nods.

BARRIE: For you don't think I'm a good man. For you think I'm closed and cold. For you think my sentimental attachment to your boys is unnatural in ways you can't fathom, and maybe you could if you were a more learned fellow. But in your heart you feel it's not right.

ARTHUR nods.

BARRIE: Still you hope that your boys are strong enough to stand on their own two feet and be the fine young men they are going to be, no matter what I do.

ARTHUR nods.

BARRIE: But now we're up against it and we can't do things by halves. This room will be closed and shuttered soon, and no one will come in… And what becomes of the boys? Who's to pay for school? Who's to keep up the house and staff? … Who's to be their father now?

ARTHUR nods.

BARRIE: Are you giving them to me, Arthur?

Beat.

ARTHUR nods.

BARRIE: Free and clear?

ARTHUR nods.

BARRIE: Would you say it?

ARTHUR: Yes.

BARRIE: Yes, what, Arthur? I need you to say it. I'm so sorry. I must hear it.

ARTHUR: My boys…my boys…my boys…are yours.

Beat.

BARRIE: Peter, take your father out. Mark him now. That's a good man there. You'll rarely see his like, and never his better.

PETER PAN leads ARTHUR away.

PETER watches BARRIE.

PETER: What did he feel? He had got exactly what he wanted, but he wasn't triumphant. He wasn't crowing like Peter Pan over the body of Hook. Maybe grown ups don't crow.

ALICE: What do you feel?

PETER: Like I turned the first page of a book.

ALICE: What's the book called?

PETER: The Morgue… I don't run from the tears. I know that's part of life. Not the crocodile tears of a fairy story, but genuine mourning… <u>Anguish</u>… Shall we go on? There's more.

ALICE: No. We needn't.

PETER: Alice in Wonderland is bolder.

ALICE: She was younger.

PETER: More resilient?

ALICE: More uncaring.

PETER PAN: *Wendy, when you are sleeping in your silly bed you might be flying about with me!*

ALICE*: Ah, the dear old days when I could fly!*

PETER PAN: *Why can't you fly now?*

ALICE: *Because I am grown up, dearest. When people grow up they forget the way.*

PETER PAN: *Why do they forget the way?*

ALICE strokes his hair gently.

ALICE: *Because they are no longer gay and innocent and heartless.*

PETER: *(To BARRIE.)* … If only that were true. I wasn't heartless. I felt everything too much.

BARRIE: You didn't know yourself as boy.

PETER: Of course I did.

BARRIE: No, you remember yourself as you are now, only smaller.

PETER: It was my life, I remember it.

BARRIE: You weren't the man you are.

PETER: And I was heartless?

PETER PAN: I'm not heartless.

BARRIE: You were never one to cry.

PETER: What does that mean?! What does that matter?!

PETER PAN: Crying isn't for pirates!

PETER: Not like I didn't feel anything.

ALICE: But did you feel enough?

PETER PAN: If I'm sad on Monday I never remember it on Tuesday, so why bother in the first place?

PETER: God, it's all I can do nowadays to keep from crying! Sometimes I think I'll go mad from all the tears. Like a ridiculous little girl… *(To ALICE.)* … Like <u>you</u>, drowning in a pool of your own tears!

ALICE: Not me. Alice.

ALICE IN WONDERLAND: Me?

BARRIE: This makes me very sad, Peter.

PETER: Good, you deserve to be! I don't mean that.

BARRIE: At the grave of your father I looked over the faces, the five of you… And you, Peter, cheeks dry, so stoic… Beautiful and wounded.

PETER: As beautiful and wounded as Michael?

BARRIE doesn't respond.

PETER calms down.

PETER: I wonder… Was I old enough to understand what death was? Things go away and don't come back? That made no sense. Peter Pan always came back. A tap at the window and there he was. That's what you taught me, Uncle Jim.

BARRIE: Not a tear for your father.

PETER: I've cried about it since.

BARRIE: <u>Or your mother</u>.

Difficult beat.

PETER explains to ALICE:

PETER: It was only three years after my father died. My mother fainted one afternoon, right there in the parlor, her arm fell, I remember that, fell to the carpet and stretched out towards me. Her maid cut her stays so she could breathe. I don't remember if the bone was iridescent, sorry. In any event, we forgot all about it… And then it happened again… It was cancer. Again.

ALICE: I am so sorry…

PETER: We were cursed. Like something from one of his melodramas: the family curse… At least she went quickly, with minimal disfigurement, which she would have found intolerable… And from then on, we were his.

BARRIE: My boys.

PETER: To exploit.

PETER PAN: To immortalize!

PETER: What child wants to be immortal?!

ALICE: What child thinks he isn't?

PETER: Did you think you were going to live forever?

ALICE: I still do.

PETER smiles.

ALICE: May I ask a personal question?

PETER: You seem incapable of asking anything but.

ALICE: Were you interfered with?

PETER: Molested you mean? By Barrie? No, nothing like that… Not <u>physically</u> anyway.

This strikes a chord with her.

PETER: To be asked to reckon with things beyond your years? Is that to be molested? … To be fixated upon. To be kept too close.

ALICE: To be forced into feelings you don't understand. To be spoken to about emotions too strong for youth, too deep for childhood.

PETER: To always disappoint because you don't love back enough.

PETER PAN: You love back as much as you can, that's all.

ALICE: To be the dream child in a dream you couldn't possibly comprehend.

ALICE IN WONDERLAND: Nor should you, because you're only a child.

ALICE: <u>Being made to grow up too soon.</u>

PETER: Yes. That's it. We've arrived.

ALICE: Where?

PETER: At our story… At Peter and Alice.

ALICE: The love story?

PETER: Partly… And partly that other book. The endlessly painful one with no happy ending.

ALICE: Honestly! I gather it's fashionable among young people to be dreadfully grim and depressive, you wear it as a badge of pride, but it's rather a bore. Now I've had my share of difficulties, but I've always carried on with some hope.

PETER: "Difficulties" you call it? That's a comfortable euphemism, like finding another word for cancer.

ALICE: Loss? <u>Death</u>? Is that what you want to hear?

PETER: That's what it is.

ALICE: I'm not afraid of the words, but I don't luxuriate in them.

PETER: Is that what I do?

ALICE: I think so.

PETER: That's just who I am.

ALICE: It's indulgent.

PETER: Sorry.

ALICE IN WONDERLAND: Stop arguing, it's too boring!

PETER PAN: Or start fighting at least! Who has a sword?

PETER: *(Continuing to ALICE.)* All right then, let me ask you: these feelings of loss, do you remember the very first time you felt them? … And were you the same person after?

ALICE: How can I remember something like that? It's too vague.

ALICE IN WONDERLAND approaches.

ALICE IN WONDERLAND: Now she's telling stories.

PETER PAN: I love stories! Are there Indians?

ALICE: I'm not telling stories.

ALICE IN WONDERLAND: Of course you are! You remember perfectly.

PETER PAN: And pirates and monsters and ships and battles and motorcars and balloon trips and undersea creatures and…!

ALICE IN WONDERLAND: The darkroom, silly!

This stops ALICE.

CARROLL: <u>Alice, keep still</u>!

ALICE IN WONDERLAND: Don't you remember the darkroom?

PETER: Tell me.

ALICE: No.

CARROLL: <u>You must stay exactly as you are</u>!

PETER PAN: I love stories more than anything. Wendy told stories. And then she grew up.

PETER: Tell me a story, Wendy.

ALICE looks at him. So be it.

ALICE: My sisters and I had gone to Reverend Dodgson's studio to be photographed. This was not uncommon; we'd done it many times...

CARROLL: You must hold still, Alice!

ALICE poses for a picture. CARROLL is photographing her; a painstaking and elaborate process in 1863.

ALICE IN WONDERLAND strikes an identical pose.

CARROLL goes about the minutiae of his task.

ALICE: I smell the chemicals still... Bromide and chloride dissolved to make the solution for the negative... Then like magic out comes the polished glass plate, which had to be perfectly clean, I've never seen anything cleaner, no dust, no imperfections, like the skin of a baby, fresh like youth, I don't know like what, like <u>innocence</u>!

PETER: *(Laughs.)* Oh God!

ALICE: Don't make me laugh, I'm supposed to be standing still... Then he carefully brushed the solution on the glass with a darling little sable brush I always coveted.

ALICE IN WONDERLAND: *(Re: sable brush.)* Oh! It's ravishing!

CARROLL: Don't move! Just a little longer.

ALICE: Then he whisked the plate into the darkroom to dip it into the silver nitrate and then so gingerly back into the camera, like a surgeon those hands, those soft hands, then a final adjustment to the lens… *(To CARROLL.)* … I want to move.

CARROLL: You'll ruin it all.

ALICE: Lorina's making faces!

CARROLL: She's a very silly goose and you're my Queen! Hold still, Queen Alice!

ALICE: Then the moment! Hold your breath! Lens cap off. Time… stops.

Everyone holds their breath.

A few frozen moments.

ALICE: Lens cap on! Move!

CARROLL: Come with me, Alice! Double quick!

CARROLL and ALICE hurry into the darkroom.

Light almost disappears. They are now lit by the muted glow of the darkroom.

ALICE: Into the darkroom! Shut the door. Like being lost at the bottom of the ocean, submerged in the deep dark.

PETER PAN: With the sea creatures!

ALICE IN WONDERLAND: Are you happy now?

ALICE: The plate eased into the solution of acid and sulphate…back and forth, back and forth… What could be more thrilling than to see the negative gradually take shape, <u>yourself</u> gradually take shape?

ALICE IN WONDERLAND: There you are… But in reverse, topsy-turvy, like everything in Wonderland. You and not you.

ALICE: Even now, all these years later, the odor of certain chemicals brings me back there, to that room, on that day… This was the second and final time we were alone.

CARROLL: Look, I'm starting to see you…

ALICE: Can't my sisters watch?

CARROLL: The door's shut now. We'd ruin everything… There's your face emerging…

ALICE: I don't know that I like my expression. I seem a bit dour.

CARROLL: You seem precisely you, precisely now. It's this moment, captured forever, never changing.

ALICE: Only it's that moment back there and I've already changed.

Beat.

CARROLL continues to develop the picture.

CARROLL: Do you think you'll change much as you get older?

ALICE: I should hope so. Who wants to remain the same forever?

CARROLL: Do you think you'll remember me?

ALICE: I don't know.

CARROLL: Ah.

ALICE: I'm bound to meet lots of people in my life, and some very memorable. I should think you would be one of the most memorable, but I can't say for certain.

CARROLL: It's a fleeting time, this we have… When you're like you are now.

ALICE: You mean when I'm eleven?

CARROLL: P-p-p-partly that.

ALICE: Is that why you take so many photographs? So you won't forget?

CARROLL: I'll never forget. But you will. You'll move on to your adulthood of ways and means, of fancy dress balls and that bluff good fellow you're going to marry, all the things that will make up the sum of your life. And a happy life it will be I know... But no reason to be sad for me. For I have this, don't I?

ALICE: But that's not me... I know that's not really me.

Beat.

He continues to work on the picture for a moment.

CARROLL: You're coming along nicely... You see how you are? ... Never growing older, never growing wiser... Like in my heart.

ALICE: *(To PETER.)* I didn't understand fully.

PETER: But you understood enough.

CARROLL: I have a wish for my child-friends. Do you know what it is?

ALICE: That we always stay like we are. But I don't understand why.

He stops.

He considers whether to go on.

CARROLL: In the place called Adulthood, there's precious few golden afternoons. They've gone away to make way for other things like business and housekeeping and wanting everyone to be the same, just like you, all the lives lived in neat hedgerows, all excess banished, all joyous peculiarities excised. It's grim and shabby. There are no Mad Hatters and there are no Cheshire Cats, for they can't endure the suffering of the place.

ALICE: Please stop...

CARROLL: That's the p-p-p-place called Adulthood... I'm there now. You'll be there soon enough. And you'll never leave... But here and now, in this room, and on this glass plate, and in the story I'm writing, you'll never be there...

And you'll never be hurt. And you'll never be heart-sick. And you'll never be alone… You will be beloved.

ALICE is near tears.

ALICE: I have to go.

CARROLL: It'll ruin the picture.

ALICE: May I go?

Beat.

CARROLL: Go, Alice.

She quickly leaves the darkroom, moves away from CARROLL, trying to recover her equilibrium.

PETER PAN: *(Disappointed.)* That was an awful story!

ALICE IN WONDERLAND: Shhh.

ALICE looks at CARROLL.

ALICE: Poor wounded soul. Everlastingly tormenting himself about a sin that didn't exist, but was completely true… I think the photographs were just a way to give him a safe framework to explore some unknown and dangerous landscape. He transformed his desires into paper and silver nitrate. What could be more innocuous?

PETER: Perhaps we all do that when we grow up. Find safe ways to make dangerous trips.

PETER PAN: Generally the pirate lagoon is more dangerous than the Indian camp.

ALICE IN WONDERLAND: Except when it's the other way around.

PETER PAN: Exactly! … It'll be dark soon. Help me find some wood for a campfire.

PETER PAN and ALICE IN WONDERLAND assemble a campfire.

ALICE: I went home that day and told my mother of our conversation in the darkroom. What I could understand of it… She didn't let us see him after that. She made me burn all his letters. All that special purple ink he used, up in flames... A year later I received the manuscript of "Alice's Adventures Underground" in the post. In his own hand, with his own drawings... I never thanked him.

PETER: And you never saw him again?

ALICE: Much later. When I was grown and married. We had tea with my sister Lorina... We were cordial strangers... The golden afternoon was over. I thought it was going to be endless. But it was as quick as the beating of a dragonfly's wing.

PETER PAN and ALICE IN WONDERLAND ignite their representation of a campfire.

ALICE and PETER are drawn toward it as well...it suggests CARROLL's letters burning, the smoke drifting up.

They all huddle by the fire, it's warm and intimate... We're in a beautiful representation of Neverland now.

ALICE: Lord, as many days as are left to me, I'll never forget those letters burning... It was the cruelest thing I'd ever seen: all the lovely words, all his heart's devotion, <u>gone.</u> As if they never existed... It was the first time I realized that things don't always stay the same... *(she watches the smoke drift away)*... There it goes; into the vapors... Should life really be that delicate?

PETER: Life was supposed to be strong and hearty. Like a pirate.

ALICE IN WONDERLAND: But sometimes it's gossamer, like Tinker Bell.

PETER PAN: Like a Mock Turtle's tear... It gets cold at night in Neverland. He didn't write about that.

PETER PAN shivers, a little chilled.

PETER unconsciously puts his arm around him.

ALICE IN WONDERLAND: There is no night in Wonderland. No one sleeps much.

PETER PAN: The Dormouse sleeps… The Mad Hatter I think.

ALICE: Would the Mad Hatter dream about being sane?

PETER: Believe me, he would.

ALICE: And Peter Pan, what would he dream of?

PETER PAN: Mother.

ALICE takes in the lovely fire, the stillness, the beautiful nighttime setting.

ALICE: It's enchanting here.

PETER: Oh yes…

He wanders forward, holding PETER PAN by the hand.

PETER: Neverland is enchanting; it always was to me… I remember the first time I saw the play. I thought it was all real, you remember?

PETER PAN: Yes.

PETER: I thought you were real and Captain Hook was real and the painted flats were endless vistas.

PETER PAN: Aren't they?

PETER: If they were you would have flown off forever, never to be seen again, onto the next…enchantment.

He leaves PETER PAN and steps forward alone.

PETER: I wanted to live there, Mrs. Hargreaves… From my box, the first time I saw the play, my brothers at my side, Uncle Jim busy somewhere backstage, I saw Neverland come to life. It was real. It was real… And it was so beautiful… I could fly.

PETER PAN: You can.

PETER: After the performance Uncle Jim took us backstage. It was a mad bustle, even that was thrilling. I mean I knew it wasn't <u>actually</u> real, I knew they were all actors, and we were in a theatre… But I needed to know if this place existed, if it were somehow <u>true</u>, even though it wasn't real.

So as the party was going on and everyone was celebrating I wandered onto the stage by myself. Just me… How large it was… I saw the painted backdrop of Neverland. The pirate ship…the wooden moon… And I closed my eyes and spread my arms… And it was true.

ALICE: Through the looking glass…

PETER: For a moment… Then I opened my eyes and heard the party, and Uncle Jim calling me, and my brothers laughing… And life went on.

ALICE: But it was true.

PETER: When I was a child.

Beat.

ALICE: So was Wonderland. I could chart every foot of it. But the depths of Mr. Carroll, those anguished letters… Those were the Jabberwocky, the dangerous, impenetrable things.

PETER: Uncle Jim wrote letters too, compulsively, hundreds of them. He poured out his heart to us.

ALICE: He did love you.

PETER: Oh yes. But it was a melancholy kind of love, because it was always entwined with an inevitable sadness. He knew we were going to grow up and leave him alone… First George to Eton and Oxford and then Jack and then me and then Michael… Michael, who always set his truest course…

BARRIE: Dear Michael, The Adelphi House is haunted tonight. I think your brother's namesake is tapping at the window in search of his shadow. Sometimes I feel I'm in search of my shadow as well, but he's busy with his mannish pursuits at Eton…

PETER: They wrote to each other every single day from the time Michael went to school… Mountains of letters, oceans of words… Sometimes the separation was too much for

Uncle Jim and he would go to Eton and stand on the
fringes of the playing fields, watching him from a distance.

ALICE: Like a lover.

PETER: Like a sailor's wife waiting for her husband to return
from the sea.

ALICE: And the letters…and the devotion that inspired them…
all gone now…like a Mad Hatter's dream…smoke and
ash…a little dust in the corner of the box you keep your
toys.

She looks at PETER.

ALICE: It is a love story, as you promised.

*ALICE IN WONDERLAND hops up, breaks the mood, turning to
PETER PAN:*

ALICE IN WONDERLAND: Come here, boy! Dance with me.

PETER PAN: No!

ALICE IN WONDERLAND: Why not?

PETER PAN: Because you're very ugly.

ALICE IN WONDERLAND: No I'm not.

PETER PAN: Because I've many important things to do.
There's a staff meeting this morning and I've a luncheon
appointment at Simpson's.

ALICE IN WONDERLAND: If this is a love story there has to be
dancing.

PETER PAN: Not with me!

ALICE IN WONDERLAND: Don't you want to fall in love?

PETER PAN: When I'm old and practically dead. And since I'm
immortal, that's never, so there.

He stomps away.

ALICE IN WONDERLAND is hurt.

ALICE steps forward and offers her hands.

ALICE IN WONDERLAND looks at her, smiles and takes her hands.

Gentle music as they dance.

REGINALD (REGGIE) HARGREAVES enters crisply, like a fresh breeze. He's a good-looking, athletic, hearty young man. It is 1879.

REGGIE: Alice Liddell, you promised <u>me</u> the next dance!

ALICE turns to him, surprised.

REGGIE: What are you staring at? I've been waiting over there all night like – what? – a Labrador or some other sad sort of whathaveyou. Come on! You won't be so churlish as to renege!

ALICE: Reggie…?

ALICE IN WONDERLAND happily hands ALICE to REGGIE.

REGGIE: Before we dance, I've got to say something to you. What I mean is…well… Let's clap hands and make a go of it! Lord, what an ass I am! Sorry – didn't mean to say "ass." Blast it all! Sorry – didn't mean to say–! Look what you do to me, Miss Liddell!

She laughs. He's charming in his inarticulate awkwardness.

REGGIE: At least I made you laugh, that's something.

ALICE: You could always make me laugh.

REGGIE: I'm an absurd fellow, no use hiding the fact, as if I could, you know me inside and out, those eyes of yours just – ah, what's the word?! – Look here! I'm no scholar, that's God's truth. But I'm a more than commonly good shot and a good bat and a really top-notch spin bowler, I can speak some French, I've got an income and the estate will be wholly mine, and I'm nowhere near good enough for you, I think you might break if I touch you, not that I would ever touch you, with too much vigor I mean! But, but– <u>Blast</u>!

He peters out.

REGGIE: I've lost the words.

ALICE: Shall I find them…?

REGGIE: Please.

ALICE: I wish you to be my wife.

REGGIE: That's the second part. The first is this… *(He kneels.)* … I love you. I shall always try to be worthy of you… Say you will be my wife, Miss Liddell.

ALICE looks at him, but doesn't answer.

ALICE IN WONDERLAND: What are you waiting for?!

ALICE: At the moment… I hesitated.

ALICE IN WONDERLAND: But he's so handsome!

PETER PAN: *(To ALICE IN WONDERLAND.)* That's the sort you like: thick-headed kneeling gallants. I'll never kneel to anyone!

PETER: Why did you hesitate?

ALICE: I suddenly saw it as a compromise. I would be giving up too much… It was like I was my mother, watching Lorina put on her first corset: resignation to something vast, and helpless to change it.

REGGIE slumps. He's disheartened.

REGGIE: Not much of a lark anymore, is this?

ALICE: Reggie –

REGGIE: I'm terribly sorry, Miss Liddell. Forgive me… *(He stands, proceeds with some difficulty.)* … I know you've been raised with certain expectations. You've been around scholars all your life; men of learning and polish. Surely that's what you always imagined for yourself… And I know myself, that's not me, never will be… I had hoped, I see now foolishly, that there was more to life.

Beat.

REGGIE: I'll bid you goodnight.

He starts to go.

ALICE IN WONDERLAND: Wait!

He stops.

ALICE IN WONDERLAND: *(To ALICE.)* Don't let him go!

ALICE: I wanted to be a writer when I was little, did you know that? I wanted to be an independent woman, like Jane Austen.

ALICE IN WONDELAND: He's a fine man and he loves you!

ALICE: Or a poetess.

ALICE IN WONDELAND: Look at him.

ALICE: I wanted so much.

Beat.

She finally looks at REGGIE.

ALICE: I will be your wife.

REGGIE: Do you mean it?

ALICE: Heart and soul.

REGGIE springs to her.

REGGIE: God, this is splendid! Dodged a bullet there! Now I've got to talk to your father, should have done that first. Blast! Got it all back-assed – sorry!

He kisses her, ecstatic, and bounds away.

ALICE is almost overcome.

She touches her lips.

Music builds to a glorious waltz.

ALICE: We were married at Westminster Abbey… After the wedding he took me home. The only house I ever lived in outside my father's.

REGGIE: Place is called Cuffnells, damned if I can tell you why, been the family estate back to good old King so-and-so-the-fourth. Some of the richest Hampshire earth going;

plant a stone and it'll grow... Let me present you. Shan't bother with the names, can't remember 'em myself half the time...

He introduces the parade of servants. ALICE is in awe of the grandness of the house and the lifestyle.

REGGIE: Butler, under-butler, cook, under-cook, footman, other footman, boot boy, coachman, groom, under-groom, head gardener, topiary gardener, under-gardener, and your seven pretty maids all in a row: ladies maid; scullery maid; laundry maid; kitchen maid; other kitchen maid; under-housemaid; other under-housemaid.

PETER PAN: *(To ALICE IN WONDERLAND.)* Say that three times fast!

REGGIE: You're home, Queen Alice!

A spirited waltz is heard. It's a glittering ball at Cuffnells.

ALICE: Who says Wonderland doesn't exist? Who says there are no happy endings? Had I not found mine? ... Days and nights of balls and fetes and tableau vivant on the lawns, riding to the hounds, into town for theatre and exhibitions, all those golden things that don't exist anymore, like this music, like the waltz... And then the boys! Best of all, our boys... Alan and Rex and Caryl... Our three sons growing strong and true...

PETER PAN: *(To ALICE IN WONDERLAND.)* Oh, all right! Stop looking at me with those great cow eyes!

He dances with ALICE IN WONDERLAND.

ALICE dances with REGGIE.

BARRIE dances with CARROLL.

Even PETER is charmed by the music and swirling couples.

ALICE: And if as he aged he grew more conservative in his views, tending to be a little stern, a little mean...and if he never read a book, but played golf instead...and had clumsy affairs with those seven pretty maids...and

I was the tiniest bit bored by it…by everything…and I would never be Jane Austen…and I took rather too much laudanum to sleep at all… Well, if that's growing up it held no heartbreak for me. It was not Mr. Dodgson's place called Adulthood, that darkroom horror… It was my life, and in the end my boys made it all worthwhile.

PETER: Crawling over your lap like puppies.

ALICE: <u>My children</u>. One more marvelous than the last… Alan and Rex and Caryl…

PETER: George and Jack and Peter and Michael and Nico…

CARROLL: Alice and Lorina and Edith…

BARRIE: Wendy and Michael and John…

ALICE: How could it ever end?

PETER: If we could only stay here forever.

ALICE: Stop the clock.

PETER: Close the book.

ALICE: Just one more endless summer.

The music suddenly ends as PETER PAN breaks the mood.

Boldly, to ALICE IN WONDERLAND:

PETER PAN: I'll never understand grown ups!

ALICE IN WONDERLAND: Nor I. They have perfectly good breast of guinea hen in front of them, they only want mutton.

PETER PAN: Any time they're happy, they can't wait to be sad.

ALICE IN WONDERLAND: Never here and now, always there and later.

PETER PAN: Always looking at the clock.

ALICE IN WONDERLAND: Looking over their shoulder.

PETER PAN: Then back at the clock.

ALICE IN WONDERLAND: Time for this, time for that, never time for "well, here we are, isn't it glorious?"

PETER PAN: Go to a party, look at the cake, long for the cake, reach for the cake–

ALICE IN WONDERLAND: Don't eat the cake.

PETER PAN: I love cake.

ALICE IN WONDERLAND: I love pie.

PETER PAN: He loves gin.

ALICE IN WONDERLAND: And have you noticed – they're always waiting for it to rain?

PETER PAN: They carry umbrellas on the sunniest days – which is dangerous because if you're attacked you need one hand for your cutlass and the other for your pistol.

ALICE IN WONDERLAND: Everyone knows that!

PETER PAN: Maybe they forgot?

ALICE IN WONDERLAND: Sometimes they don't even have pistols.

PETER PAN: What do they do when the Indians attack?!

ALICE IN WONDERLAND: They're always forgetting.

PETER PAN: When they're not always remembering.

ALICE IN WONDERLAND: So there's never time for tarts.

PETER PAN: Or cutlasses or kites.

ALICE IN WONDERLAND: Or croquet!

PETER PAN: Or dancing to the pipes in the deep, dark woods!

ALICE IN WONDERLAND: Like they used to.

PETER PAN: I hear the pipes all the time!

ALICE IN WONDERLAND: She wasn't always like this, mind, like she is now. She was <u>wicked</u> in her day.

PETER PAN: The old lady? Not likely!

ALICE IN WONDERLAND: That darling little sable brush? Pinched it.

PETER PAN: Good for her!

PETER: You didn't!

ALICE: Still have it!

ALICE IN WONDERLAND: And she knew men. Grown up gentlemen I mean, in her day. A lot of them.

ALICE: *(Unpleasantly shocked.)* Oh.

PETER PAN: He carries a flask and drinks all the time.

PETER: *(Quickly to ALICE.)* I told you that.

PETER PAN and ALICE IN WONDERLAND grow increasingly revelatory, but are entirely without rancor:

ALICE IN WONDERLAND: She took lovers and then grew bored.

PETER PAN: His children are embarrassed by his drinking.

ALICE IN WONDERLAND: She doesn't love all her sons the same.

ALICE: That's not true!

ALICE IN WONDERLAND: 'Tis.

PETER PAN: He's a great big liar too. Betrays his wife regularly, pretends she doesn't know.

ALICE IN WONDERLAND: Does she know?

PETER PAN: Of course she does! He doesn't care.

ALICE IN WONDERLAND: She despises tradesmen and blackies and chinkies and pretty much anyone who's not her.

PETER PAN: He still lives on Barrie's money.

ALICE IN WONDERLAND: She bites into her pillow and cries every night.

PETER PAN: Barrie paid for the publishing house.

ALICE IN WONDERLAND: But thinks <u>other people</u> crying is weakness.

PETER PAN: Hates him, but takes the money.

ALICE IN WONDELAND: She thinks about killing herself.

PETER PAN: He's hit his children.

ALICE IN WONDERLAND: She looks at the bottle of laudanum and wonders.

PETER PAN: He fears he's going mad.

ALICE IN WONDERLAND: She's forgotten how to play croquet.

PETER PAN: <u>He's forgotten how to fly</u>.

ALICE tries to stop the scene:

ALICE: Stop this.

PETER: Mrs. Hargreaves…?

ALICE: We need to stop this.

ALICE IN WONDERLAND: You can't tell us what to do.

PETER PAN: Never could.

ALICE: We need to stop right now!

ALICE tries to escape. But PETER PAN and ALICE IN WONDERLAND block her way; it's like a game to them. She is increasingly distraught.

ALICE IN WONDERLAND: Is this a game?

PETER PAN: What are the rules?

PETER: *(Concerned.)* Calm down, please…

ALICE IN WONDERLAND: Maybe there are no rules!

PETER PAN: Even better!

ALICE IN WONDERLAND: And then of course she sent her sons to the war.

The music and lighting change.

It is now 1915... The trenches of France...young men off to war... perhaps the distant sound of battle.

This affects ALICE and PETER strongly.

PETER PAN is delighted:

PETER PAN: Oh well done! Now we're going to have some <u>action</u>! No more dancing! Time for some fisticuffs, my lady!

ALICE IN WONDERLAND: Boys! You're only happy with dirt on your knees and blood on your nose.

PETER PAN begins to play his pipe. The tune eventually turns melancholy.

ALICE: Is there a moment you grow up? ... Not an evolution, not the passage of a summer or a year. <u>A single moment</u>... Perhaps it was when my boys first put on their uniforms. The moment it all changed.

CARROLL: You must hold still, Alice...

ALICE: When everything fell to pieces.

PETER: Like Humpty-Dumpty.

ALICE: Cracked apart.

PETER: Into a thousand pieces.

BARRIE: To fight, and fly, and fight again...

ALICE: The whole fiction of my comfortable life.

PETER: Never to make sense again.

ALICE: <u>Never</u>.

PETER PAN: I don't know that word.

ALICE IN WONDERLAND: It's a twelve-year-old word in truth.

PETER: Once the war came, everything you thought you knew...

ALICE: <u>Was wrong</u>.

PETER: The answer is yes. There's a moment. One day I killed a man, you see. In the deep, dark woods. The forest was choked up with bodies and mud. I was knee deep in it. If you step on a body you can split the stomach and release the gasses, and the stench is appalling, so I was looking down, trying not to step on any corpses, I looked up and the fellow was suddenly just there in front of me and I shot him…

ALICE: I sent my boys off to the war. So handsome in their uniforms. So smart they were.

PETER PAN: *How clever I am. Oh, the cleverness of me.*

PETER: I didn't even know if he was a German, his uniform was so muddy. I just shot him in the chest. I was so scared… I sat down on the ground and watched him die. I knew he was dead when he didn't move, but the fleas did. They crawled away from him, like they knew, like they were abandoning him, it was so sad… I sat on the ground and I watched him die… Then I went mad.

ALICE IN WONDERLAND: *But I don't want to go among mad people!*

PETER PAN: *Oh, you can't help that. We're all mad here.*

ALICE IN WONDERLAND: *How do you know I'm mad?*

PETER PAN: *You must be. Or you wouldn't have come here.*

PETER: Shell-shock they call it, but it wasn't a shock. It was a numbing. I felt absolutely nothing as my life cracked open and spilled out of my head, started pooling around my feet… I was seconded home, in shame. I went to asylums. Light bulb never off: suicide watch. Rubber mouth guard so I wouldn't bite my tongue off… But my life was still pooling around my feet. I couldn't stop it. I was all cracked open.

ALICE: I saw my boys go away to war… And everything that had ever happened in my life led me to believe they would return.

ALICE waits.

ALICE IN WONDERLAND goes to ALICE, wiser than her years:

ALICE IN WONDERLAND: *That was the last time the girl Wendy ever saw him. For a little longer she tried for his sake not to have growing pains... But the years came and went without bringing the careless boy; and when they met again Wendy was a married woman, and Peter no more than a little dust in the box in which she kept her toys...*

The moment has come.

It's inevitable.

PETER PAN: Third Battalion barracks. Company C. 10th May 1915... Officially reported that Captain Alan Hargreaves killed in action 9 May 1915 please to convey deep regret and sympathy of their Majesties the King and Queen and Commonwealth government in loss that parents have sustained in death soldier reply paid Colonel Boscombe.

ALICE is shattered.

PETER PAN: ... officially reported that Second Lieutenant George Llewelyn Davies killed in action 15th March 1915 please to convey deep regret and sympathy...

PETER: *And all the king's horses, and all the king's men...*

PETER PAN: ... officially reported that Captain Rex Hargreaves killed in action 25th September 1916 please to convey deep regret and sympathy...

ALICE is going to collapse.

ALICE IN WONDERLAND quickly brings a chair.

ALICE sits.

She is lost in herself.

PETER as well.

ALICE IN WONDERLAND wanders into the no-man's-land of the war.

A beat as she takes in the desolation…and then turns to CARROLL tenderly:

ALICE IN WONDERLAND: In the place called Adulthood there are no Cheshire Cats…for they can't endure the suffering of the place.

CARROLL steps to her.

Beat.

He bows deeply.

CARROLL: Queen Alice.

He begins to leave the stage, but…

ALICE IN WONDERLAND: Mister Dodgson…

He stops.

She bows to him.

He is touched by the gesture.

He then leaves the stage, and the story.

Beat.

MICHAEL DAVIES enters. He's a beautiful and poetic young man, fragile.

ALICE IN WONDERLAND: My, he's handsome… Maybe he'll dance with me.

PETER PAN: He won't.

ALICE IN WONDERLAND: Who is he?

PETER PAN: Michael… My shadow.

PETER: *(To BARRIE.)* You used to stand on the fringes of the playing fields, watching him…

BARRIE: I cannot picture a summer day that does not have Michael skipping in front. That is summer to me…

PETER: Uncle Jim… White or black?

Beat.

BARRIE: Black.

BARRIE and PETER sit, play chess. MICHAEL hovers near them, he's nervous about something.

They are in BARRIE's palatial flat at the Adelphi Terrace, where MICHAEL lives when he's not at Oxford. It is 1921.

MICHAEL: Uncle Jim, I'd thought I'd bring my friend Buxton up to town next weekend. I think you'd like him.

BARRIE: I need a pipe.

MICHAEL: Let me.

He cleans, prepares and fills BARRIE's pipe during the following. It's quietly domestic.

PETER: Your move.

BARRIE: You're thinking strategically.

PETER: Played a lot in the war. And not too much else to do in the nutter hospital.

BARRIE: I wish you wouldn't talk like that.

PETER: Sorry, "sanitarium." Oh yes, that's much better.

MICHAEL: *(Continuing to BARRIE.)* I know you don't always approve of my mates from school but Buxton's your sort, not a playwright I mean, but <u>exceptional</u> really. Sort of a poet, I guess.

BARRIE: Do what you wish, Michael.

MICHAEL: That means you'd rather I didn't.

BARRIE: It means nothing of the sort.

PETER: A poet?

MICHAEL: Sort of a poet, yes.

PETER: What sort?

MICHAEL: I meant he writes poetry.

BARRIE makes a move on the chessboard.

PETER: You're not thinking.

He quickly takes a piece.

They play for a moment as MICHAEL continues to prepare BARRIE's pipe.

BARRIE: *(To MICHAEL.)* Only I see you so rarely.

MICHAEL: So you'd rather I didn't bring him?

PETER: Oh just bring him!

MICHAEL: Not if Uncle Jim doesn't want me to.

BARRIE: I've no hold on you, Michael, you're twenty years old, do as you like.

MICHAEL: Oh God!

PETER: Just bring him!

MICHAEL: I want you to meet him. It's important to me.

BARRIE: Why?

MICHAEL: Because he's my friend.

BARRIE: Your "poet" friend.

MICHAEL: I suppose.

BARRIE: You've a lot of friends.

MICHAEL: Do I?

BARRIE: And now a "poet."

MICHAEL: Yes, I–

BARRIE: What next, I wonder?

PETER: *(To BARRIE.)* Don't.

MICHAEL: Look – It's because I – I want you to know him. It means something to me that you know him.

BARRIE: What are you trying to say?

MICHAEL: We've talked about going away, that's all.

BARRIE and PETER stop.

PETER: Going where?

MICHAEL: France. Paris… To study painting.

BARRIE: You'll do no such thing.

PETER: Painting?

MICHAEL: Yes! Painting! I want to study painting. Buxton says I've got some talent and we ought to chuck it here and go off to Paris for a while and make a go of it.

BARRIE: I won't hear a word of it. You're being childish.

PETER: Stop it.

BARRIE: *(Ice.)* I'll speak my mind in my own house if you'll allow me that… *(To MICHAEL.)* … You've got to finish your studies and be a practical man. You've got to grow up, lad. Do you think I'm going to pay your tradesman's bills forever?

This strikes like an arrow.

BARRIE: I've no interest in pictures myself. Don't see the point of them. Lot of cloud-spinning, I've always thought. But if that's what you want to do, live that sort of life… <u>Bohemian</u>… Is that what you'd call it? … Michael… <u>Bohemian</u>?

MICHAEL: I don't know.

BARRIE: Whatever you call it, who am I to stop you? Do what you will. I don't need to meet this "poet" of yours.

MICHAEL is near tears.

BARRIE: I'll have my pipe now.

MICHAEL hands him his pipe and quickly moves away from the scene; upset.

PETER PAN impulsively goes to comfort him. The lights change as they move away, isolated in their togetherness.

ALICE: *You ought to be ashamed of yourself, said Alice, a great girl like you to go on crying in this way! Stop it this moment, I tell you…*

PETER PAN: *But she went on just the same, shedding gallons of tears, until there was a large pool all around her, and reaching half down the hall…*

ALICE: *Her first idea was that she had somehow fallen into the sea…*

ALICE IN WONDERLAND: *However, she soon made out that she was in the pool of tears that she had wept…*

MICHAEL: *I wish I hadn't cried so much, said Alice. I shall be punished for it now, I suppose, by being drowned in my own tears.*

BARRIE: Dear Arthur, Every year since your death I have written to tell you of your sons and their progress through life. I've tucked the letters away into a neat bundle, tied with a ribbon. Never did I think I could have a more difficult composition than that of 1915 when we lost George…

Light like rippling water begins to isolate MICHAEL and PETER PAN.

BARRIE: But this year, in the month of May, 19th of the month, Michael and his friend Buxton went to Sandford Pond, a few miles south of Oxford. Perhaps you recall it? It's a place where many of the boys swim…

PETER: I went there later, Mrs. Hargreaves. The water is placid.

BARRIE: They stepped into the water together…

PETER: Witnesses saw two men holding each other, not struggling, quite still in the water…

PETER PAN: *The most haunting time to see the mermaids is at the turn of the moon, when they utter strange wailing cries; but the lagoon is dangerous for mortals then…*

BARRIE: The distance from bank to bank is too small for the question of swimming capacity to enter into it at all…

MICHAEL: *Two small figures were beating against the rock; the girl had fainted and lay on the boy's arms. With a last effort, Peter pulled her up the rock and then lay down beside her. He knew that they would soon be drowned…*

ALICE IN WONDERLAND: *Wendy was crying for this was the first tragedy she had seen…*

PETER PAN: *Peter had seen many tragedies; but he had forgotten them all…*

PETER: *The rock was very small now; soon it would be submerged…*

BARRIE: They were not struggling. They were not trying to save each other…

MICHAEL: *By and by there was to be heard a sound at once the most musical and the most melancholy in the world: the mermaids calling to the moon…*

BARRIE: Or maybe, Arthur, in the end they did save each other…

PETER: *Peter Pan was not quite like other boys; but he was afraid at last…*

ALICE: *A tremor ran through him, like a shudder passing over the sea…*

MICHAEL: *But the next moment he was standing erect on the rock again, with that smile on his face and a drum beating within him…*

PETER PAN: *To die will be an awfully big adventure!*

Lights change.

BARRIE stands in shock.

PETER is in his own thoughts.

ALICE has remained seated.

PETER: And you wonder I call it a <u>lie</u>? … That play… That book.

ALICE: Oh yes, it's a lie.

PETER: Maybe there was a time I believed it, but life, Mrs. Hargreaves…

ALICE: Oh yes.

PETER: Peter and Alice… Shards of youth… I'm no more Peter Pan than you're Alice in Wonderland. We are what life has made us.

He looks to BARRIE.

PETER: Even he finally had to realize the same thing I have: the only reason boys don't grow up is because they die… Isn't that true, Uncle Jim?

Beat.

BARRIE: It is.

He leaves the stage, and the story.

PETER: There are no mermaid lagoons; there are still, deep waters where lonely boys drown themselves. There are no pirate captains; there are trenches and bullets and razor wire. We do not fly, Mrs. Hargreaves, nor could we ever.

PETER PAN: Speak for yourself!

PETER: Stop it.

PETER PAN: Don't you ever get tired of blaming me for your miserable life?

PETER: You're the glass that distorted everything.

PETER PAN: Honestly! I fly through the night, skip on the clouds, sing in the forest, fight me some pirates, what harm have I ever done you? If you're broken, you broke yourself. I won't even remember you tomorrow.

ALICE: You talk to him like he's real.

PETER PAN: I am real!

PETER: He's not.

ALICE: Hard to tell sometimes.

PETER: <u>Not for me</u>.

ALICE IN WONDERLAND: But then you think you're going mad.

PETER PAN: We're all mad here.

PETER: Be quiet!

PETER PAN: Someone get him his mouth guard.

PETER: He doesn't exist! – *(To ALICE IN WONDERLAND.)* – Neither do you! This is demented.

PETER PAN: You're the expert on that.

PETER: None of this is real.

ALICE: I wonder who's more real, Peter Davies or Peter Pan?

PETER PAN: Bully for her!

ALICE: In a hundred years no one will ever remember Alice Liddell. And no one will ever forget Alice in Wonderland... Now you tell me who's more real.

PETER: Mrs. Hargreaves... We can't live in a fantasy. <u>Reality may be hard, but it's all we have</u>.

ALICE IN WONDERLAND: *Wendy felt at once that she was in the presence of a tragedy...*

PETER: Maybe there was a time but... The war ditched me really, and then Michael's death. The nightmares are pretty unspeakable. You see, when I close my eyes I see them, my family...and I feel...<u>I feel they are waiting for me</u>. As if I would be <u>betraying</u> them if I didn't join them: for we are a family defined by our sadness... To this day I'm frightened to close my eyes, because when I do I see them, that line of corpses, lunging for me in the dark... My father, gaping in that monstrous leather jaw... My mother, falling in the parlor, hand outstretched... My brother George, bloody hands gripping the barbed wire tight... My brother Michael, eyes staring up, sinking down, reaching for me... I see them... Even now...<u>even now</u>...

He closes his eyes.

Keeps them closed.

PETER: Do you see them?

This is harrowing for him.

PETER: I want to hear the mermaids singing to the moon… I want to be young, with my brothers… I want to be sane again and whole… I want… I want…to jump on the wind's back and away we go…

He opens his eyes.

PETER: But here we are. Awake again. Into truth.

ALICE: I can't afford your truth. I need mine.

PETER: Even if it's not real?

A beat as she gazes at him.

She finally stands.

It's a little difficult getting up. She feels her age.

She looks at him: dead on.

ALICE: Shall I tell you about reality, young man? … When my son Alan was killed in the war, and my son Rex was killed in the war, I thought I could not know more suffering. My husband did not recover from the shock, honestly. He did not understand where his boys had gone. He got very old and I with him. He died six years ago, my gallant Mr. Hargreaves. After forty-six years of marriage.

Beat.

ALICE: It was then I learned the estate was in less than ideal shape. He had not overseen our finances with the acumen I had expected. That fell to me. I found I could no longer afford to keep the staff intact; those seven pretty maids are no more, Mr. Davies. Cuffnells is a large house and expensive to maintain, so I've closed most of the rooms and spend my days in the library, at the top of the house, where there's little heat and it's very drafty… As I told you,

I sold Mr. Dodgson's manuscript for the money. Because I had to… But what will I sell next year?

Beat.

ALICE: My son Caryl and his wife look in on me every now and then, but I bore them so they find excuses to come less and less. My father and mother are long since dead, so too my sisters, so too my friends. No one comes to visit me. I see no one. <u>I am alone</u>… Do you know what it is to be eighty years old and sick and alone? Do you know that truth, Mr. Davies?

Beat.

ALICE: And if I sit there in that room at the top of the house and I think about my life and if I shut my eyes from time to time and imagine being warm in the summer and I hear the bees buzzing and for a moment I truly am Alice in Wonderland, do you have the heart to tell me I'm not?

She advances on him:

ALICE: I can be the lonely old woman in the drafty room or I can be Alice in Wonderland… <u>I choose Alice</u>.

Beat.

ALICE: So, now the choice is yours.

PETER: I don't know what you mean.

ALICE: It's your life. Not Mr. Barrie's. Not your brother's. Yours… So choose.

PETER: What would you have me do?

ALICE: I would have you live.

PETER: Believe in fairies?

ALICE: Why not?

PETER: Dance to the pipes in the deep, dark woods?

ALICE: Take my hand. We'll go together.

She holds out her hand.

He looks at her.

At her outstretched hand.

ALICE: I'm a dying old lady, not much loved by anyone... But I know the way to Wonderland.

He longs to.

More than anything.

But he can't.

His heart breaks.

PETER: I have grown up.

The backroom of the bookshop reforms around them.

Fantasy and memory are banished.

Except...

PETER PAN and ALICE IN WONDERLAND remain with them, on the fringes, like ghosts, like shadows, watching.

ALICE hears voices off.

She glances through the door into the bookshop.

ALICE: I believe they're ready for us, Mr. Davies.

PETER: Oh...of course.

ALICE: I'll see you inside then.

She steps to exit into the bookshop.

But then she stops in the doorway, looks back at PETER.

Almost as if she has one more thing to say.

ALICE IN WONDERLAND: *(To PETER PAN.)* Two years later, Alice Liddell Hargreaves died peacefully in her sleep.

ALICE exits into the bookshop. PETER starts to follow her. He turns.

PETER PAN: *(To ALICE IN WONDERLAND.)* Some years after that, Peter Llewelyn Davies walked down into the Sloane Square tube station and threw himself in front of a train.

PETER stands for a moment, looking at PETER PAN.

PETER PAN leans forward, yearning.

PETER turns and leaves, slamming the door behind him.

PETER PAN turns to ALICE IN WONDERLAND.

Blackout.

The End.

I'LL EAT YOU LAST:
A CHAT WITH SUE MENGERS

I'll Eat You Last: A Chat With Sue Mengers was first performed at the Booth Theatre, New York on April 5, 2013, with the following cast and creative team:

Cast

SUE MENGERS   Bette Midler

Creative Team

Playwright	John Logan
Director	Joe Mantello
Scenic Designer	Scott Pask
Costume Designer	Ann Roth
Lighting Designer	Hugh Vanstone
Sound Designer	Fitz Patton
Associate Director	William Joseph Barnes
Production Manager	Juniper Street Productions, Inc.
Props	Kathy Fabian
Stage Manager	Laurie Goldfeder
General Manager	101 Productions, Ltd.

Producers
Graydon Carter
Arielle Tepper Madover
James L. Nederlander
The Shubert Organization
Terry Allen Kramer
Stephanie P. McClelland
Jeffrey Finn
Ruth Hendel
Larry Magid
Jon B. Platt
Scott and Brian Zeilinger

Warning

This play contains profanity, smoking, alcohol consumption, drug use, and gossip.

Characters

SUE MENGERS

Setting

The living room of Sue Mengers' Beverly Hills home...1981.

This play should be performed without an intermission.

Dedicated to Brian Siberell and James Bagley
who I believe would eat me almost last.

Curtain up to reveal...

*The living room of Sue Mengers' Beverly Hills house...
Pale colors, pale flowers... Tasteful and designed.*

*SUE MENGERS relaxes comfortably on her luxurious sofa. She
wears one of her signature caftans and wire-rim glasses. There's
a coffee table before her with a dish of chocolates, an ashtray,
and some objects d'art.*

She smokes, constantly.

*She looks at the audience, a gaze at once baleful and mischievous.
And always there's the wicked sparkle.*

SUE: I'm not getting up... It's my house, you get up.
Only don't. I just had the carpet cleaned for the
party. Don't take offense but the carpet is for the
guests tonight. You will be long gone by then. Oh
yes, long gone and back to Van Nuys or wherever
you hail from, by way of too many freeways I'm
sure, poor lambs, I'm weeping for you already.
Honestly, you see that tear?

So forgive me for not getting up. Imagine me as that
caterpillar from *Alice in Wonderland*; the one with
the hash pipe. He didn't need to get up. He could
sit there and look over his domain and torment that
little brat. He was a smartass for sure, but he had
some brio. Lemme tell you, all that worm needed
was a three-line phone and he could have been the
best agent in Wonderland... Yes, you notice the
phone.

There's a phone on the table next to her.

Now it's not my normal practice to have a phone in
the living room. I think it's rude to be in the middle
of some <u>fascinating</u> conversation with a starlet about
which plum role she's trying to get – meaning which
director she's trying to screw to land said plum
– and all of a sudden the phone rings and before
you know it you're embroiled with the travails of a
client. Movie stars never have problems; they only
have <u>travails</u>... So the phone is usually banished to
other parts of the house. But tonight I'm expecting
an important call... Yes, you all know, The Call.

We might as well talk about the elephant in the
room.

A glance to the audience: I dare you.

I'm on the edge of my seat, metaphorically
speaking, for the call that will bring the dulcet tones
of Ms. Streisand to my ears. It will come when it
will come, Barbra-time being elastic and elliptical.
I'll let it ring twice or even three times if I'm feeling
cheeky and then we'll <u>dish</u>. I love a dish with
Barbra. She who came up with me. She who is my
good right arm. She who is me if I'd had any talent.
She of the nails and the voice and now the perm,
which we will <u>not</u> discuss. She who fired me today.

No, to be accurate, her lawyers fired me. Her
microstate of serious Jews that joined arms and
bottle-danced their way to the speaker-phone
and pressed my button... Speaker-phone, what a

villainous invention. All the intimacy of a proper phone call gone. All the purring seduction of setting the phone on the pillow next to you replaced by "What? Who said that? Which kike am I talking to?" ... I had one of those new car phones installed once. Size of a dismembered baby's torso. Well, I tried using it but it took all the fun out of driving around trying to run over Faye Dunaway...

So the firm of Mandelbaum, Schwartz, Speer and Goebbels promised me Barbra would call me herself tonight. I wait. All on pins and needles. Can't you tell?

> *She grandly brushes her hair back, a signature gesture, very Veronica Lake.*

You like the place? My modest little hacienda in the Hills of Beverly. Previously owned by Miss Zsa Zsa Gabor, a star of the highest magnitude. For weeks after moving in I was finding little bits of marabou and sequins. Everywhere you looked: marabou and sequins. Like she shit them. So after having the house fully de-sequined I had my queens come in to decorate. Tip from Sue: if you're not particularly domestic yourself, as I am not, you want the place shrieking with queens. Don't get in the way, let them flutter.

Actually I did have one argument with my decorating boys. They insisted on putting in the pool. You cannot have, they averred, a Beverly Hills

mansion without a pool. You will lose the respect
of your friends and neighbors. You will lose tiles in
the great Mah Jong game that is Hollywood. So I let
them put in the fucking pool… *(She gestures vaguely
behind her.)* … It's out there somewhere. I'm not
really sure. "Exercise" doesn't play a big part in my
life. By this time your Sue has embraced her inner
zaftig.

She laughs; a low, wicked, delightful sound.

*Then she takes a chocolate from the little dish on the
coffee table before her. Eats it. Yum.*

Besides, my husband loves a little jiggle. Ah, yes,
my beloved spouse. Jean-Claude Tramont's his
name, Belgian, yum. He's what we call a hyphenate:
writer-director-producer. Generally in Hollywood
the more titles you attach to your name the less
successful you are. But fair enough, he's in the
game like everyone else. We're one of those typical
Hollywood couples: on a good night we're Nick and
Nora Charles; on a bad night we're Nick and Nora
Charles Manson.

But I love him to little tiny pieces. And the only
thing I love more than my husband is my <u>dinner
parties</u>. Is there anything more sublime than hosting
twelve of your nearest and dearest for an evening
of good chat? That's what we do here: <u>we</u> <u>dish</u>.
Who's in, who's out, who's up, who's down, who's
on bottom, who's on top but really wants to be

on bottom. It's the most delicious gossip you ever heard. I love gossip, don't you? 'Tis like mother's milk to me, and it's the lube by which this town slips it in. Whole place would grind to a slow, agonizing dry hump without gossip… Like I always say: if you can't say anything nice about someone, come sit by me.

She laughs.

Okay, that wasn't me. That was Alice Longworth. Or Halston. Who remembers? It doesn't matter. You hear a good story you claim it like a conquistador planting the flag, honey. Most of the stories I hear about myself are sheer fantasy, as are most of the stories I tell about myself. But why use your own boring stories when stealing your friends' is so much more fun? And in Hollywood there's no such thing as stealing anyway. Oh no, not at all. When Brian DePalma rips off Hitchcock it's not theft – it's homage. We pay a fuck of a lot of homage out here.

For all you simple homemakers out there, like me, here's the big secret to a successful dinner party: only invite movie stars. They won't come, but you'll have made the effort.

You cannot imagine the pleasure I get casting the parties: looking out over the glittering landscape of Hollywoodland and Broadwayville, seeing who's out of rehab and might need a drink, checking on

the latest star signed with another agent I need
to steal… Only thing is, all my guests have to be
<u>famous</u>. Honey, my own mother couldn't get in
if she were standing outside in the rain… It's all
Twinklies here! I love my stars! I love 'em! So when
I'm planning a party I go into conclave and give it
a good old think, then I send out the white smoke
and the invitations are issued hither and yon. But
Sue has to be careful because…<u>it's all business</u>.
Everything in this town is business. We're a
company town and anyone who tells you otherwise
is misinformed.

Right in there, at my table, deals are brokered;
careers come to life or die untimely deaths.
There's not a dinner I give where I'm not trying
to get a client a job. It's one long audition. I seat
the delightfully hyphenated Ann-Margret next to
divinely talented Mike Nichols and she's in *Carnal
Knowledge* by dessert. Burt Reynolds shares a beer
with Alan Pakula and he's landed *Starting Over*.
Lauren Hutton meets Paul Schrader and walks away
with *American Gigolo*. I love it! I love my job!

But I really only have two hard and fast rules about
throwing parties, which you are encouraged to
employ:

Rule Number One: All showbiz all the time. Don't
talk to me about politics, science, sports, or animal
husbandry, I don't give a shit. The only thing I
care about is movies and movie stars. Nothing

will make me snooze faster then some goddamn celebrity opining on matters global. Honestly, Henry Kissinger is only interesting to me because he's fucking Jill St. John. … Now back in what we dinosaurs refer to as "the sixties" everyone had to get deeply political. Suddenly all the stars were wearing headbands and getting awfully earnest about Attica or Kent State or Cambodia. Is there anything more boring than Cambodia? No one shoots a movie there. No one vacations there. Can I find it on a map? Do I own a map? What the fuck are these people talking about?! … *(Pretends to fall asleep.)* … Zzzzz. … I just don't understand why anyone would talk about anything other than show business. I don't care what it is. Vanessa Redgrave comes over once and she's sitting there, downing glass after glass of my best Veuve Clicquot like a good Socialist, chattering on about Palestine or the grape boycott or whatever the hell it is and finally I just scream: "Jesus Christ, Vanessa! Cut to the chase! Is Richard Harris a good fuck or not?!"

And Rule Number Two: No children. The only exception I ever made was for Tatum O'Neal after she was nominated for her Oscar. The Oscar nomination instantly makes you a Twinklie… I just don't get the appeal of "children." This one client squeezed out an infant and wanted to bring it by the house. I told her: "Why don't you drive past and let it wave?" … Now Sigmund Freud – or better yet Monty Clift playing Sigmund Freud – would

probably say my aversion to kids has something to
do with my childhood.

She glances at the phone:

And since we appear to have some <u>time</u>, I'll tell
you about that. Once upon a time I was born in
Germany and…wait…for this I need fortification.

She looks around… Spots a little silver box on a table
across the room… No way she's getting up.

Then she scans the audience. She selects a man.

You… Yes, you, honey. Come on up here. Sue
needs you. Don't be shy. You're never going to
make it in this town without some initiative. This is
your big break, baby.

She finds an audience member to play along. Hereafter:
The Unlucky Audience Member.

The Unlucky Audience Member heads to the stage.

Stop… Weren't you listening, honey? … The carpet.
Lose the shoes. Thanks.

She makes the Unlucky Audience Member take off his
shoes.

No, we'll wait. It's not like we have anything else to
do. Tick tick tick.

When his shoes are off…

Now could you be a sweetheart and get me that silver box?

The Unlucky Audience Member gets the silver box… Brings it to her.

Thanks, you're a doll. You may sit down again. Take the shoes. Don't be a stranger.

The Unlucky Audience Member gets his shoes and returns to his seat.

SUE opens the silver box. Removes a joint and lights it.

Ahhh.

I was born in Germany, a couple years ago. When I was eight Mr. Hitler started getting stroppy so my parents decided it was time to seek greener pastures. We packed up what we could carry and joined the ranks of sensible Jews who were getting gone. This was my father, my mother and me. … It was all pretty much like the Von Trapps in *The Sound of Music*, only without dreamy Christopher Plummer and all those not-up-to-their-usual-standards Rodgers and Hammerstein songs.

We settled in Utica, New York, where my playboy father quickly discovered there wasn't much of a market for émigré German playboys. He was a feckless sort of man, honestly, but we had to eat, so he ended up as a travelling salesman, which didn't make him scream with joy.

I didn't speak a word of English so the first few years were grim. I remember at school always feeling outside looking in, you know? I would stand there on the playground and watch the other kids playing together, not twenty feet away. The most popular girl was called Gladys Burton. She was the ringleader, the <u>star</u>. I looked at her. What did she have that I didn't? Why her and not me? … Longest twenty feet there ever was… But I was too embarrassed by my accent to talk to her, to even make the effort. The fat little German Jewess? Come on… I eventually learned English, almost entirely through the movies. Lessoned by Joan Crawford and Bette Davis and Joan Blondell in little fleapit bijous across Utica, I picked it up. That's why I still talk like a gum-cracking Warner Brothers second lead. Once I had the rudiments of the language, I knew I had to make the effort. Night before I practiced saying it over and over: "Hello, my name is Sue Mengers. Hello, my name is Sue Mengers. No accent. No accent. Hello, my name is Sue Mengers." Next day at recess I walked across the playground… Maybe the bravest thing I ever did… I go up to Gladys Burton.

"Hello, my name is Sue Mengers."

And she was nice. Thank God for that. My life would probably have been entirely different if little Gladys Burton had been a bitch.

So a couple years later my father kills himself. He wasn't sick and he didn't leave a note. He killed himself in a Time Square hotel room, which seems redundant.

She takes a hit on the joint.

We never knew why. Well, living with my gorgon of a mother might have had something to do with it... But looking back I think it was this: his life was never going to align with his self-image. He was never going to be the soigné gentleman he imagined. It wasn't going to be cigarette boats on Lake Como; it was going to be third-class trains and cold-water flats until the credits rolled. He died of thwarted dreams, my dad... And you wonder why I work so hard for my clients?

Well, my mother couldn't stand the shame his suicide heaped on us in little old Utica so we bid farewell to Gladys Burton and escaped to big old New York City, where every third person is a fat German Jewess and nobody gives a shit about anything. We settled in the Bronx and it wasn't long before my obsession with movies and movie stars led me to the inevitable conclusion: I had to be an actress! I had to! How could I not be part of those ravishing fantasies that gave me the very language

I speak?! Why couldn't I be as sleek as Lauren
Bacall? Why couldn't I crackwise like Rosalind
Russell?

But to be a movie star I figured I should at least
have a passing acquaintance with the art of acting…
A notion a surprising number of our current movie
stars seem hell-bent to disprove… So I signed up
for a six week evening class at the Lizzie Borden
School of Elocution and Rhetoric on 45th and Lex.
First night of the class I get all dolled up in my
cutest number, take twenty-seven trains in from the
Bronx, and walk up the fabled stairs at 45th and
Lex to seize my destiny… One look around… Holy
shit! Everyone is prettier than me, even the boys. I
felt like Judy Garland at the MGM School: on one
side there's Elizabeth Taylor and on the other side
there's Lana Turner. I mean. Fuck! … There goes
that dream.

She laughs.

But was your Sue deterred? No she was not. If
the stage door was closed, there was always a
window to jimmy open and scamper through. I
started reading the trades looking for my window.
In this life, kiddies, there's always a window. Ah
ha! I answered an ad for a receptionist at the
William Morris Talent Agency and scampered on
through. As a secretary I answered the phones
and I made coffee and I listened. I listened to
every conversation I could, sometimes through the

keyhole it must be said. I found out I loved it: I loved the business of the business. Why be a king when you can be a kingmaker?

She lights another cigarette. She's a two-fisted smoker: joint in one hand, cigarette in the other.

So there I was, a little pisher making 135 bucks a week, but I had a desk and a phone and damn if I wasn't going to get noticed. Flashing the William Morris name like an FBI badge, I went everywhere and met everyone. Night after night I was out pressing the flesh, charming my way, going to shows, going to dinners. Pretty soon people were asking about that cute little blond who seemed to know a lot of people and had opinions about which she was not shy. And she was kind of funny too, which was unusual in a city crammed with humorless Radcliffe dykes.

What was I doing? Crossing the playground. "Hello, my name is Sue Mengers, William Morris Agency."

You want to be a thing? Make yourself that thing.

We were all making ourselves up then. Not just me. Case in point: … Now this may come as a shock to you but every single person who works in the theatre is gay. Without exception. So I was not unduly surprised when a client invited my boss and me out for a drink at a gay club. Frankly, it had been a long week and I didn't want to go. But your

Sue couldn't face the Bataan Death March back to
her Bronx walk-up without a canteen of sustenance,
so I went. Place was called The Lion... *(Glance to
the Unlucky Audience Member.)* ... You remember, the
place on 9th Street... There was a singer that night.
Her name was Barbara Streisand. Barb-a-ra. She still
had the other "a" then, that's how early this was...

SUE imagines the scene.

She gets up there on this tiny stage with one little
spotlight, this funny-looking girl, all Second Hand
Rose, she shuffles around awkwardly, checks her
mike a few times, nervous chatter from her, people
are talking, no one gives a shit...

Then out of the corner of my eye I see her do
something I'll never forget. I'm sure no one else
noticed it. She makes the guy adjust the spotlight.
Like this forty watt spotlight with an amber gel in
the middle of this shitty gay bar. She makes him
move it until it's the way she wants... She took
the time to make a little magic. That's what a <u>star</u>
does... Now she's got my attention... And then she
sings.

Beat as she muses.

After the show I marched up to her with all the
subtlety of a Panzer division rolling into Poland.
"Listen, kid, you're gonna go the distance. I can
see it. The rest of them, these fucking jamokes,

they can't. But I can. And I wanna be there… *(She smiles and extends her hand.)* … Sue Mengers, William Morris Agency."

She looked at me. She took my hand.

Beat.

She picks up the phone… Listens for the dial tone.

CALL ME, YOU CUNT!

She places the phone down and continues amiably:

Anyway, back to me… The great day finally came when the big window opened. A young guy named Tom Korman with his own talent agency offered me my own desk. He took a chance I might make an agent. God Bless Tom Korman! Without Tom Korman, there's no Sue Mengers. Where would we be without those people who believe in us, those brave souls who take a second to glance our way and say, "What the fuck, why not?"

Korman and Associates – that's me, the associates – was a second-tier agency at best but goddamn it, I was an agent at last! I went to work doing what an agent does, which is essentially two things: signing and holding. You sign the talent and you hold on to them. In between – when time allows – you get them work. You talk them off the various ledges of show business. You make them happy. You make them rich. You get them laid. You Sherpa up the side of any mountain they choose. And along the way – oh please god! – you have some laughs… Now after all that time as a secretary I was straining at the leash to start building my client list. I went after everyone. Honey, I was so ambitious I would have signed Martin Bormann. I signed Julie Harris instead.

Add her to the list: Gladys Burton, Tom Korman, and Julie Harris. She's a great actress and a great friend. If you haven't seen her in *Member of the Wedding* you have denied yourself one of the true highlights of movie acting… My very first client. My only client for a while… And she taught me a lesson I've never forgotten: you have to speak to the artists in their language, not yours. Julie talked to me about Shakespeare and poetry, about drama of substance, because that's what mattered to her. She wasn't interested in box office receipts or boosting her quotes. When I spoke with venality, her eyes glazed over… After our first meeting I went to the Public Library every day on my lunch hour and I read Ibsen and Aristotle and Odets. The smile on Julie's face the first time I quoted poetry. That smile I'll treasure until my dying day.

Because here's the truth of agenting: you are the public face of the client. You're representing them literally and figuratively. A great agent is a great chameleon: you have to become the client's mirror. That's the reason clients leave mostly: they no longer like the way the agent is presenting them to the world. Anyone with balls can make a cold call to David Merrick and bully and swear and play hardball. It takes a great deal more finesse to make those calls with sensitivity and nuance. When you call to get Julie Harris a job you don't say: "Listen, you motherfucker, give this bitch the part." You call, you make a sound like you're sipping tea; and you say "Good afternoon, Miss Julie Harris is considering a guest appearance on *Bonanza*, shall we discuss that?"

Then…the phone rings.

SUE jumps.

She lets it ring once…twice…a devilish glance to the audience…three times…

She finally answers, casually:

Tramont residence… Sissyyyy, hello! You're so sweet to call. You got a phone there on the farm I take it. That's a step in the right direction. How is every little thing? … *(She mouths "Sissy Spacek" to the audience.)* …uh-huh, uh-huh. Yeah, that's swell. Honey, we gotta talk about your representation. You know everything comes across my desk and I'm looking at the scripts out there and I'm sitting here worrying about you, I am, I'm fretful. There's a new Brian DePalma script nobody but me has seen that screams you and … *(Listens for a beat.)* …

uh-huh, uh-uh. Well let me tell you about it first and then I'll sleep easily, totally selfish. Now don't tell a soul but Brian's remaking *Scarface* with Al Pacino and this could be a career-changing part for you. Sissy Spacek in *Scarface*, what could be more perfect!? … *(Listens for a beat.)* …uh-huh, uh-huh. I know you just won the Oscar, but that was last year, honey. What about next year? Don't you want two? Listen, I'll send the script, you call, we talk, and we're wearing Balenciaga at the Dorothy Chandler this time next year! … *(Laughs, listens for a beat.)* …uh-huh, uh-huh. That's not all. I don't mean to speak ill of any other agents but I gotta be honest with you: I don't think your guys are thinking big picture. By which I mean recording… *(She smiles, she knows she's hit a nerve: gotcha.)* … So I was talking to David Geffen about how great you sounded in *Coal Miner's Daughter*. "Why is this girl not under contract, David? Why the hell isn't she cutting albums left right and center? Now don't tell anyone because the release doesn't go out until next week, but David just signed Donna Summer for his label, which is stratospheric, right? Why couldn't you be next? Who couldn't build a label with Summer and Spacek?! … *(She listens for a beat.)* … Well you don't have to do what she does. You could do what you do. That folk singing thing you do. I'll call David tonight, honey. Point is that Sue loves you and Sue's thinking about you and I would die for the chance to represent you because– *(She listens for a beat.)* … uh-huh, uh-huh, uh-huh. What? Oh my gosh! You just stop right there! I would never try to poach a client from another agency! Never, ever! You should forgive that I'm concerned about your career and– *(She listens for a beat as she eats another chocolate.)* …uh-huh, uh-huh… Listen, no one understands fidelity more than I do. I'm not saying that the fine gentlemen at CAA can't do their jobs, it's just that– *(She listens for a beat, getting more worked up now.)* …uh-huh, uh-huh… Baby, you do what you want, Sue's always here, in your corner, life is long. But really, honey, isn't it time to shit or get off the pot? You're hot, I'm hot, town's hot, time's now, which I'm afraid your pseudo-Ivy-League-whiz-kid-boy-agents-slash-rentboys will fail to recognize. So you give it a good hard think, kid, and use your goddamn head. Smoke a joint, pluck a chicken, drive to the Piggly-Wiggly, whatever the fuck you do to relax, and consider what I am now saying to you: the most powerful talent agent in the entire fucking world is putting out her hand and you slap it away at the peril not to our friendship, which is unassailable, but to the peril of your immortal soul, or at least your immortal career, and singing career, and next Oscar, and Grammy, and everything I know will come your way, but only if you drop the Holly Hobbie bullshit and start acting like the strong, talented, decisive artist you are, or would want to be if any of those motherfuckers at CAA ever let you know you could be! Which you can! With me! Right now! Ciao, baby!

She hangs up.

She brushes back her hair, very ladylike again.

I've been trying to steal Sissy for years… In my
long pursuit of Miss Spacek I actually made
the pilgrimage to that farm she lives at. It's in a
mythical land called Virginia. So I get all dolled
up in my cutest little Chanel number and fly to
Middle Buttfuck where there's this guy waiting
for me in a jeep. Lemme tell you, Sue does not
do jeeps. General Patton does jeeps. But I'm on
a holy mission so I get in and endure the ride to
Sissy's "farm." I can only surmise it was a mud farm
because that's all there was. I get out. Sink three
inches. Chanel pumps stay behind as I tip-toe over
to meet Dame Spacek who's all dressed in early
Waltons. Then she proceeds to give me a tour of
the "farm" which only results in mud up to my
twat. Finally we retire to her house and have a cup
of tea, herbal, natch, and I proceed to tell her how
much her prick of an agent is ruining her career and
I hope she sees a future in mud farming because
that's where she's heading if she doesn't leave said
prick and sign with me. She's vague and moon-
beamy and promises to keep in touch. I get back
in the jeep, back to the airport, back to LA, leaving
a little trail of dried mud flakes snowing from my
twat.

Moral of the story: when you're trying to steal a
client, you do anything. So you lose a pair of savage
little Chanels; the commission on Sissy Spacek pays

for a whole boutique... The big picture, my friends.
The big picture.

You note I have no shame about saying I'm trying
to <u>steal</u> Sissy. We're all headhunters in my business.
It's a tough old game, Hollywood. Survival of the
fittest... Favorite book I never wrote: *I'll Eat You
Last: A Cannibal Love Story.*

She smiles and lights another joint, or cigarette, or both.

Now all these invaluable lessons about the
byzantine ways of the Movieland Empire I learned
when I finally made it out here to LA in 1968. By
now I'm working for Freddie Fields and David
Begelman at the company that became ICM, my
current home.

At first I was a little frog in a big pond so I had to
work at it. I had to get noticed.

Riding to the rescue on her white steed came
Barbra Streisand, who it should go without saying
has never been on a horse in her life, so I speak
figuratively. Barbra don't do livestock.

Here we were; two klutzy gals from the outer
boroughs amidst the lotus blossoms. The big
difference is that by then she was a major star and
I'm still low down in the credits. So Barbra started
schlepping me along to parties... "I'm gonna bring
my friend Sue... You mind if I bring my friend Sue

Mengers, you'll love her"... Being on Barbra's arm immediately gave me clout. Heads turned. People started to pay attention. There was a certain freak appeal for sure: women agents were almost unheard of. And a woman agent who drank and swore and knew what she was talking about and looked fucking adorable? Come on, I was made for this place!

What Barbra did was open the window for me. Once I was inside, it was up to me. So I went to work. I talked to everyone. I was persuasive, I was funny. Most of all, I was ferocious. To me "no" always meant "maybe."

Case in point: Gene Hackman.

Gene was an early client of mine, an early believer, and one of the best actors I know; incapable of being false on screen. We hear about this movie. It's perfect for him, the next rung up the ladder. It's the part of Popeye Doyle in *The French Connection.* I try to land it but Gene's never opened a movie as the lead, and he doesn't scream movie star handsome, so it's the definition of a <u>hard sell</u>... I go to work. I start calling. I'm on the phone five times a day to Billy Friedkin, the director. I'm on the phone hourly with Fox, the studio. They tell me "no." I hear "maybe." Meanwhile they're offering it to everyone in town. Paul Newman turns it down. Steve McQueen turns it down. Robert Mitchum turns it down. James Caan and Peter Boyle turn it down. I'm pitching for Gene like a motherfucker with every pass. Cha-ching: No sale.

Then one morning my spy at Fox tells me they're about to offer it to…wait for it…this is true… Jackie Gleason.

Well this is the last fucking straw, right? Now they're just slapping my tits! I stomp out of the house, get into my Bentley, light up a joint, and drive straight over to Billy Friedkin's house like a Valkyrie in heat. I pull up and park right in his driveway. I mean there's no way he can get out past me. I wait. He comes out to go to work.

"Billy, you're splitting my brain open over this goddamn picture! Is this a joke?! Jackie-fucking-Gleason?! What, was James Coco not available?!"

He says, "No, no, no, Sue, that's not right, we're not offering it to Gleason. We're about to make the offer to Charles Bronson."

This is a tactical error. He's told me something I don't know. This is the first I've heard of Charles Bronson. And fuck! This is bad. Bronson's a box office star and he'll take it…

I improvise but quick:

"Billy, Billy, Billy, think about this for five minutes. Popeye Doyle is a hulking Neanderthal of a character. You cast Charles Bronson and you've cast a hulking Neanderthal... <u>Where's the irony</u>? ... You want a guy who <u>looks</u> like a brute, but inside the eyes you see feral intelligence. This is Gene Hackman! Smart as a whip, educated, former Marine, classical actor, did you see his Konstantine in *The Seagull* in New York? Fucking heart-stopping performance; broke your heart." ... A part I have no idea if Gene Hackman ever played, by the way ... "You cast Charles Bronson everyone says 'Look, there's Charles Bronson' and they stop believing in the story. It's just another Charles Bronson vehicle. But if you cast Gene Hackman you get someone the audience <u>doesn't</u> know, someone they'll <u>believe</u>, someone who just might not win: the underdog. You get that big, ugly potato face with the soul of a Beat poet. This is your Popeye Doyle!"

It's in his eyes. He's starting to see it. I take the shot:

"Listen, just hold the offer to Bronson five minutes and meet Gene, see if I'm not right. One measly sit down is all I ask. Call it a favor to me. You don't click, fine, you make the offer to Bronson and everyone's happy, most of all me. Whattaya think?"

He says, "Come on, Sue, would you move your car?"

"Not until you tell me you'll meet with Gene."

I light a cigarette. A very long cigarette.

He sighs. "Favor to you. That's all."

I say, "Baby, you're the best."

Year later Gene and Billy pick up their Oscars…
That's how you do the job, kids.

She smiles, loves a happy ending.

She picks up another chocolate… Puts it down…
Immediately picks it up again and eats it.

Pretty soon you can see how I was getting the
reputation of an agent who fought for my clients;
who wasn't afraid to take on the big boys. The
trickle of clients became a flood. After Gene came
Candy Bergen, Mike Nichols, Michael Caine,
George Segal, Herbert Ross, Anthony Newley,
Dyan Cannon, Bob Fosse, Sidney Lumet, Burt
Reynolds, Cybill Shepherd, Ryan O'Neal, Rod
Steiger, Peter Bogdanovich, Gore Vidal, on and on.

She puts her feet up on the coffee table, sinking deeper
into the sofa.

So in the blink of the proverbial eye, I'm living the
life I always dreamed about… I'm Bette Davis. I'm
Ava Gardner. Sometimes I'm Broderick Crawford,
but still… Point is: I'm not just Barbra's friend, I'm
Sue Mengers. People took my calls instantly: the
only real measure of success in Hollywood by the
way.

I'm the toast of the town. Clients are getting rich. I start getting press. Mike Wallace does a piece on me in *60 Minutes*. I'm not just representing stars; I <u>am</u> a star… Cue the ominous organ music.

But before all that, let me share with you the Five Golden Rules of being a great agent.

> *She realizes her glass is empty…glances over at the sideboard across the room loaded with liquor… No way she's getting up.*

> *She looks again to the Unlucky Audience Member, in her baby voice:*

Honey, Sue's thirsty.

> *She shakes her empty glass.*

Come on, baby, you're on again.

> *She makes the Unlucky Audience Member return to the stage.*

> *If he doesn't remember about his shoes, she reminds him to take them off:*

Shoes… Now go over there and bring me the Lalique decanter. Go on, chop-chop.

> *He goes to the sideboard. It's filled with different decanters.*

She purrs:

It's the tall one, dear.

The Unlucky Audience Member brings her the tall decanter.

I'd ask you to join me, but that might encourage an unhealthy familiarity. Thanks, you're a peach, truly; now get the fuck out of here.

The Unlucky Audience Member starts to go...

Wait, wait... Honey, come back here...

The Unlucky Audience Member returns...

Have a chocolate, sweetie.

She gives him a chocolate from the dish on the coffee table.

You enjoy that now. Bye bye.

As the Unlucky Audience Member gets his shoes and returns to his seat she considers him, shaking her head:

Sometimes I don't think God sent his smartest Jews to Hollywood.

SUE pours herself a fresh drink... Sips... Ahh.

So you want to be a Superagent? All you have to do is follow Sue's Five Golden Rules. The more enterprising of you will want to take notes.

Rule Number One: Never Blow a Deal on Money.

In Hollywood, money doesn't really mean anything, it's just a way to keep score… It's kind of like the Easter Bunny: nobody needs it, but it's nice when it hops into your lap and warms your cooze… Let's face it, most movie stars have more money than they could spend in a hundred lifetimes, so five or ten or fifty grand here or there doesn't really matter. What <u>does</u> matter is building a career and making the smart choices. When you're an agent you have to be a giraffe: you stand looking over the trees, checking out the predators lying in wait, and hopefully see a way to the next watering hole… And a <u>smart</u> agent knows when to take less money for a job that moves your client closer to the watering hole. Big picture, remember?

Robert Evans and Roman Polanski are casting *Chinatown*. For the female star opposite Jack Nicholson they're waffling between Jane Fonda and my client, Faye Dunaway. It's coming down to the wire. My spies at Paramount tell me they're getting ready to offer it to Fonda. I go into Great White mode. I call up Bobby Evans, who I know forever:

"Bobbeeeee, listen, this movie's going to be hard enough to make without having to deal with Jane's mishegoss, you know what I mean? You have to tell her to fuck off, honey, because you're going to lose Dunaway if you don't. Now I shouldn't be telling you this, but Arthur Penn wants Faye for his new picture, so I need an answer by close of business tomorrow or we're taking it, shitting you I am not. And we won't take a penny less than 250,000, you hear me, you prick! 250,000!"

Slam down the phone. Bobby calls an hour later:

"Mengella, I hear Faye's hard to work with."
"What?! Compared to Hanoi Jane and her legions of protesting vets? Come on! And we want 250,000, you fucker!"
"75,000 or I'm calling Jane."
"Fuck you. We're taking the Arthur Penn movie!"
"Fuck you. We're casting Jane."
Slam! Slam!

I spend an hour pretending to think about it; then I call Bobby:

"Honnneeeeeey, I spoke to Faye. She's crazy hot to work with Jack, so we'll take the measly 75,000. We got a deal?"
"We got a deal."
"And guess what? There was no Arthur Penn movie! I made it up! HA!"
"Guess what? Fonda turned us down yesterday. HA!"

She laughs.

God! I love the game! … So in this case, getting
Faye Dunaway that part to move her career forward
was worth more than the money. Looking back on
her career you can see it clearly: no *Chinatown* no
Network no Oscar. The trick is seeing it <u>before</u> it
happens: all the way to the watering hole, baby.

And by the way, Faye never liked me and I never
liked her. She stayed with me five minutes. Wins the
Oscar and then she's out: bye-bye Sue… I do dryly
note with a certain amount of schadenfreude that
her last paying job was portraying Miss Eva Peron
in a TV movie. Who's laughing now, bitch?

So: Never Blow a Deal on Money.

Rule Number Two: Never Remind Them.

Here's another reason so many clients dump an
agent once they get successful: because you remind
them of when they were hungry. When they're on
the way up, they'll do anything for you. But once
they get a taste of success, as night follows day, they
start to hate you specifically because they used to
need you.

So for fuck's sake don't compound the problem
by reminding them of the "good old days" when
you were all young and eager and up-and-coming.
Movie stars have already up-and-come; they have

came-and-are. That's why they're movie stars.
There's nothing more present tense then a movie
star. You only talk to them about the future, never
the past. And if you're representing Miss Diana
Ross – as I did – you might want to avoid saying the
following as you walk the red carpet at the Oscars
with her: "Wow, Diana, long way from the days of
blowing Berry Gordy in the back of the limo, huh?"

She laughs.

So: Never Remind Them.

Rule Number Three: Never Tell Them the Truth.

Clients always say: "Come on, Sue, give it to me
straight, don't sugar coat it." Jesus God, not a one of
them could survive a single phone call that wasn't
coated with enough sugar to make Tony the Tiger
puke! You think any of them really want to know
SOYLENT GREEN IS PEOPLE?!

No, they do not… You never tell clients the <u>whole</u>
truth. You tell them <u>just enough</u> of the truth,
carefully shaded to make them feel as young and
successful and rich as possible at all times.

So, yes, I see you sitting there very righteously
saying: "But surely, Sue, you owe them the truth."
… Okay. Try looking into the eyes of someone
you love and saying this… "You're too old. You're
not hot anymore. They want the younger version

of you. They want the thinner version of you…
No, darling, they want you for the part of the
sister…for the best friend…for the sidekick…for
the grandmother… Maybe it's time to think about
TV? Maybe it's time to think about dinner theatre?
Maybe it's time to think about retirement? … You
do not exist."

Careful… The skin of dreams is so thin. You
poke one little hole and all the air hisses out. All
movie people really have, most of them, is their
confidence. You take that away and…

She shakes her head.

Beat.

Julie Harris. You know how much I love this lady…
Recently she's not so hot. Time happens, right? *East
of Eden* is a long time ago. "Who's Julie Harris?" …
But she's desperate to play Mary Todd Lincoln in
this TV thing. I go to the mat. I try everything. I
drive over there. I talk to the network. I talk to the
director. I offer bribes. I offer deals. I go flat out.
No good… "Too old. Not sexy enough." Like that
famous sex-kitten Mary Todd Lincoln, right?! … So
I have to tell Julie. We have lunch so I can do it in
person… I'm dreading it… I tell her the director has
a hard-on for whoever they cast; nothing personal,
nothing to do with her.

She looks at me. She knows.

The smart ones always know.

Beat.

So: Never Tell Them the Truth.

Rule Number Four: Never Lie to Them.

Self-explanatory.

And Rule Number Five, the final rule: Know the Spouse.

Which brings us, invariably, to Ali MacGraw.

Ali was my favorite client ever. She's a goddess; like from another universe, she floats through ours, touching lives, making the world a more graceful place. I love her to little tiny pieces… I signed her right after she married Bobby Evans. She hits it big in *Love Story*. She gets the Oscar nomination and I get her on the cover of *Time*. She's respectful and funny and – oy – so beautiful. Ali and Bob are burning up the red carpet like nothing since Gable and Lombard. She's happy, I'm happy. What could possibly go wrong?

I'll tell you in two words… Four words… That cunt Steve McQueen.

So I'm busy playing giraffe, taking care of Ali. Maybe she's getting typecast in all these preppy parts? Maybe we should look for something different? She likes the idea of challenging herself with something new. This offer comes in: *The Getaway*. Sam Peckinpah directing. Ali opposite Steve McQueen. We grab it. They make it. She falls in love. She divorces Bobby Evans. She marries McQueen.

Nooooow… I know you're not supposed to speak ill of the dead…

She looks at the audience wickedly.

Carefully fires up a joint… Ahh.

Settles in.

Steve McQueen was a total fake. This cult of personality that's grown up around him since his death is crap. He was an abusive, alcoholic, misogynistic, loutish, pretentious, mean, mean, manic depressive. That motherfucker ruined Ali's career! He was so fucking insecure! He couldn't stand her star wattage, so he pushed her into the shadows. He makes her move into this isolated house out in Malibu and she becomes his "old lady" who's expected to have dinner on the table every night at six for Steve and his stuntmen buddies. And she did! And she did! This is Ali-fucking-MacGraw, barefoot and pregnant, waiting on that cocksucker hand and foot!

She's getting angrier in the retelling:

Of course she should have told him to fuck off!
Of course she should have fought for her career!
Everyone told her. Me loudest of all: "Why the fuck
are you letting this man take away your livelihood
and your dignity?! This is your moment, Ali, it
might never come again! You gotta be smart!"

You will not be surprised to hear that Steve loathed
me. Hated it when I called, knew I was trying to
get Ali back to work. He grunted something and
then handed the phone to her without a word,
when he didn't just hang up. Had all the manners of
Richard Speck... Early on she used to bring him to
my dinner parties. He got so nervous about being
in a room full of smart, tall people that he would
have to get stoned beforehand. Then he would just
stand in the corner, trying to look deeply brooding.
But he was a fake about that too. He didn't really
brood. He'd just scrunched up his face and try to
look deep; ended up looking like Kermit the Frog
thinking about Auschwitz.

But she loved him. This was her choice... This
was her heart. And it lied to her... You saw it
happening. It killed you.

Beat.

Or maybe this is what love looks like. Maybe it was
right for her, but wrong for me. What the hell do I

know? When the clapping stops, I'm not exactly an expert on much of anything.

Beat.

So day comes I have to have it out with Ali. She's choosing not to work and the offers are drying up. If she's going to salvage her career she's got to get back to work. Rest of your life, baby, you in or out?

I drive out to Malibu… I'm nervous… I adore this girl. I'm readying every argument in my head. I'm going to have to give her both barrels, which is what you do for people you love; you give it to them stone cold. She can take it…

She slows, remembering the moment…

I pull up… She walks out of the house to meet me. Her son Josh is on her hip…

She smiles… She's <u>radiant</u>… I look at her…

"Are you happy, Ali?"

"Yeah, Sue, I am."

I give her a kiss. I turn right around and drive away. I try not to look back.

Beat.

Final Rule: Know the Spouse.

Beat.

She takes off her glasses, rubs her eyes.

She puts the glasses back on, like armor.

Not that I had all that much time to worry about
Ali, because I'm in the Barbra Streisand business.
When you're in the Barbra Streisand business
it ain't part time, and there are no weekends or
holidays... Here's what most people don't get about
Barbra: she's wicked smart. She's also what they call
a "perfectionist." There's no detail too small. She
walks in here right now she'll have rearranged the
pillows and moved all the furniture in ten minutes,
or she'd have you do it. The whole world's her
stage and she's constantly adjusting the spotlight,
you know what I mean? ... It's not for vanity; it's
for artistry. ... She's got that rarest of things in
performers: she's got taste.

About everything but which parts to play... Jesus
Christ, I battered my poor head black and blue
against the wall trying to make her take the right
roles. I argue, I beg, I cajole, I threaten, I weep.
She won't be rushed. She won't be manipulated.
She knows her worth... So she turns down *Cabaret.*
So she turns down *The Exorcist.* So she turns down
Klute. What does she want to play? A girl who
dressed like a boy so she can study Talmudic law for

fuck's sake! She drives you crazy. But still you love
her. You should hate her, but you love her. I don't
know how she does it.

Sometimes your job is just to make her laugh. Or
calm her the fuck down.

Back in '69 when Charlie Manson and his family
were getting particularly madcap with the cutlery,
she goes bananas. She's absolutely sure she's next
on the hit list. She calls me in a panic:

"Sue. I know I'm next. These people hate Jews.
They'll kill anyone. What should I do? Should I
move? Should I get a gun? Should I hide? Should I
convert? Oh mighty God I know I'm next!"

I said, "Don't worry, honey, they're not killing stars,
only featured players."

She laughs.

She glances at the phone.

I'm sure she went to those motherfuckers at CAA.

For you civilians out there, CAA is Creative Artists
Agency, the fastest rising of the so-called New Wave
agencies; the shape of things to come we are all
breathlessly promised. They've built the agency
on a puritanical screed of complete dedication:
an Armani-clad samurai culture of monkish

sublimation of the individual to the corporate entity, to quote their mentor, Stalin… Oh did I say Stalin? I meant Mike Ovitz.

No, Mike's a good boy. The kind of guy you'd loooove to get stuck on a lifeboat with. Never forget the first time I sat with Mike. He's getting all hot talking about "turnaround negative cost pickups" and "merchandizing synergy against backend residual options on a sliding scale of first dollar gross." It's like some language I don't speak he's making up as he goes… He's honestly more interested in who's making what than who's screwing who. One of us is in the wrong town… Finally I interrupt the accounting lesson to say, "But, Mike, honey, do you actually <u>like</u> movies?" … This makes him blink… I ask him, "What's your favorite movie?" … I can see the wheels spinning. Literally inside his forehead I can see the little bumps as the gears turn. He's trying to give me the answer he thinks I want; the answer that won't lose him any status, nothing too commercial or he'll seem frivolous, nothing too arty or he'll seem pretentious. He finally narrows his eyes to cold little slits and says… "*Bambi*."

She laughs.

I lose about a client a month to CAA. So does everyone… I've seen the future. And, kids, it's not a lot of laughs.

Beat.

But, hell, I figure if I can survive both Adolph Hitler and *All Night Long* I can survive anything… *All Night Long*…the movie… You know, my <u>husband's</u> movie? … Of course you've all seen it?

She gazes sternly over the audience for a beat.

All the trouble with Barbra really began with the infamous *All Night Long.* So Jean-Claude's trying to set it up for himself to direct. It's about a depressed middle-aged guy working the nightshift in a drugstore in the Valley who falls in love with a local gal. It's the kind of quirky little character movie they don't make anymore. Nary a superhero or light saber in sight. About which I can only say this: what the fuck's an Ewok?! I mean those smashed-in faces that look like gaping twats? Come on!

Anyway, this movie ain't *Star Wars* and Universal ain't gonna make it without some kind of name attached, so I start working on Gene Hackman. Gene does depressed middle-age better than anyone, right? And he owes me from *The French Connection.* Gene's a mensch and signs on to play the lead. Universal is over the moon they got Hackman in this runt of a picture. They cast Lisa Eichhorn as the gal. They start shooting. They stop shooting. It's not going well. Turns out, surprise, surprise, Lisa Eichhorn is no Glenda Jackson. Rushes are dire.

Studio's unhappy. Miss Eichhorn has to go. Gene's miserable. Jean-Claude's desolate. Sue goes to work.

I call Barbra and tell her I have a movie for her. She's in the middle of writing her cross-dressing Jew movie, so she could use a break. She says yes.

Now, in <u>retrospect</u>, this wasn't the wisest call I ever made. Is it just possible audiences won't want to see La Streisand playing a bored Valley hausfrau in this oddball movie? This question I did not ask myself. Que sera sera.

I start negotiating for Barbra and I play tough with Universal. She's white hot coming off *The Main Event* and her album "Guilty" is top of the charts. The studio knows this could be a magic moment, so they bite the big bullet. Biggest bullet there ever was. I get Barbra 4.5 million and 15% of the gross for 27 days of work. It's the most an actress has ever been paid. The town is stunned. They make the movie. *Gone With the Wind* it is not. It cost around 10 mill, ends up taking in 4, which, wags point out, is less than Barbra's salary… Look, movies fail all the time, it happens every day. But this was a <u>public humiliation</u> for Barbra Streisand. And for me.

You feel the backlash like a Malibu wildfire. Whispers that roar. "Sue Mengers forced her clients into her husband's movie." "She betrayed Streisand." "She lost Hackman." "The arrogance." "Serves her right." … Before long the whispers turn into headlines. They see blood in the water. Suddenly I'm vulnerable.

And they all wait gleefully for the giant to fall.

So maybe I was off my game. Maybe I was overconfident. Maybe I forgot my own rules. Who the fuck knows? … Maybe when I crossed the playground and said "Hello, my name is Sue Mengers" Gladys Burton looked back and said "Used to be."

So big deal. Clients leave. They've been leaving for a while actually. Peter Bogdanovich goes. Candy Bergen goes. Burt Reynolds goes. Cybill Shepherd goes. Sidney Lumet goes. Michael Caine goes. Gene Hackman goes… Ali goes… Julie Harris goes… Barbra…

Beat.

Hey, it's part of the job. I'm signing new clients all the time. And we'll all be–

The phone rings.

SUE jumps.

She answers almost immediately:

Tramont residence… Oh, Richard, hello! Honey, I'm just on the edge of my seat to see you tonight –

figuratively speaking because I'm actually ass-deep
on the sofa just a teeny-weeny bit high… *(She listens
for a beat.)* …uh-huh…oh… *(She's surprised at what
she's hearing.)* … Hey, don't give it a second thought.
We'll miss you, honey. You rest up and we'll see you
next time. Bye bye, love.

She hangs up.

Beat.

Her hand rests on the phone for a moment.

Richard Dreyfuss cancelled for tonight. Richard
Dreyfuss. Cancelled.

Beat.

The implications of this are profound to her.

She lights another joint or cigarette.

You ever seen that movie *The Poseidon Adventure*?
I have. Goddamn that's fine entertainment. And
I took particular relish in seeing so many former
clients being drowned. I don't want to spoil it for
you but the conclusion is very uplifting… Only the
B-stars survive… Just like life.

Beat.

I'll tell you, in my more lucid moments I think about getting out of the game. Leave showbiz, split this town. Give up the dinners, the parties, the openings; the whole magilla.

I think when I retire I'll take a trip to Israel. Maybe I'll go with Barbra and she can out-Jew everyone. That would be fun. We would laugh… I guess that's what's changed about Hollywood most. We used to laugh more. Honey, we used to have fun.

But the New Hollywood is upon us. Yeah, partly it's a matter of style. These new agents aren't assaulting Billy Friedkin in his driveway. They're polite, subtle men who don't work on intimidation and aggression. They don't shout, they purr. They don't attack, they finesse. They're not angry… With me you get all the crayons in the box, even the ugly ones, even the angry ones. But never boring.

Trust me; you'll miss me when I'm gone.

Beat.

She glances at the phone ruefully. Shakes her head.

Typical.

She checks her watch.

Okay, kiddies, this has been a joy, I'm faint from the sheer ecstasy. But now Sue has to get ready

for the big party with all my lovely Twinklies.
Yes, believe it or not, I must be made even <u>more</u>
beautiful. My squadron of stylists, primpers and
morticians will arrive shortly. Don't bump into them
on your way out.

She braces herself and then…

<u>*She stands.*</u>

Ta-da.

She looks over the audience.

Of course I would ask you to stay but…well…look
at you.

She nods to the Unlucky Audience Member:

You've got some potential, honey. Keep at it,
nowhere to go but up. Maybe TV.

*She slowly jiggles toward the exit. It's a major production
number.*

She stops at the doorway out.

Turns back to the audience.

One last tip from Sue… Go ahead, cross the
playground. What have you got to lose? After all,
the credits roll sooner than you think.

She's about to exit when…

The phone rings.

She looks at it… A thousand miles away by the sofa.

She glances to the audience. Hell no.

She laughs.

Now get the fuck out of my house.

She exits as "Stoney End" by Barbra Streisand is heard.

And the curtain falls on the wonderful world of Sue Mengers. Here and then gone. Never to come again.

The End.